AF872131

The Essential Retirement Tax Strategy Guide

How to Minimize Taxes on Your Retirement income and Avoid Costly Tax Traps

Susan Delaney

Table of Contents

Chapter 1: Understanding Retirement Taxes: The Essential Foundations 7

Chapter 2: Mapping Your Income Sources: Knowing What Triggers Taxes 14

Chapter 3: Tax Traps to Avoid: Common Mistakes That Erode Savings 26

Chapter 4: Smart Withdrawal Sequencing: Stretching Your Nest Egg with Taxes in Mind 36

Chapter 5: Roth Conversions and When They Make Sense 47

Chapter 6: Tax Bracket Management: Using Margins to Your Advantage 58

Chapter 7: Medicare, IRMAA, and Other Means-Tested Costs 67

Chapter 8: Annuities, Life Insurance, and Insurance Alternatives Explained 78

Chapter 9: Advanced Strategies: Backdoor Roths, Qualified Charitable Distributions, and Tax-Planning Tweaks 89

Chapter 10: Building Personalized Tools: Worksheets, Calculators, and Templates 100

Chapter 11: Case Studies and Step-by-Step Scenarios .. 110

Chapter 12: Choosing Advisors and Ongoing Learning: Staying Tax-Savvy in Retirement 121

Conclusion.. 130

Disclaimer

This book is intended for educational and informational purposes only and does not constitute financial, investment, tax, or legal advice. The information provided is based on general principles and publicly available sources as of the time of writing and may not reflect the most current laws, regulations, or individual circumstances.

Retirement accounts, tax rules, and financial strategies can vary widely based on personal factors such as income, age, employment status, location, and changes in legislation. Before making any financial decisions, including those involving 401(k) plans, IRAs, investments, withdrawals, or tax strategies, readers should consult with a qualified financial advisor, tax professional, or legal professional who can assess their specific situation.

The author and publisher make no guarantees regarding financial outcomes and disclaim any liability for loss, damage, or adverse results arising directly or indirectly from the use or application of the information contained in this book. Past performance of investments or strategies discussed does not guarantee future results.

By reading this book, you acknowledge and agree that you are solely responsible for your financial decisions and outcomes.

Copyright

For information, contact:
Susan Delaney
publishing@essentialretirementguide.com

eBook ISBN: 979-13-992704-5-7

Paperback ISBN: 979-13-992704-4-0

First published 06/2026.
Printed and bound in the United States.

A message to the reader

If you're reading this, you've likely spent years — maybe decades — building your retirement savings.

Now a different question is taking shape: how do you turn what you built into income that lasts?

Maybe retirement is a few years out. Maybe you've already stepped away from work. Maybe you're somewhere in between, still working out what comes next.

At this stage, the questions get sharper:

Will my savings last as long as I do?

How much can I safely take out each year — and how much of that will the IRS actually let me keep?

What happens if markets drop, or inflation runs hot?

Am I using my money efficiently, or just hoping it works out?

If those questions sound familiar, you're not alone. Most people are taught how to save for retirement. Almost nobody is taught how to live on those savings once taxes enter the picture.

You don't need a complicated strategy or a crystal ball for the market. You need a clear understanding of how retirement income actually gets taxed — and how to make decisions with what you've already built, instead of guessing.

This book was written for that exact moment: the one where saving is mostly done, and the real question becomes how to keep more of what you've saved.

Let's start with how your money gets taxed once it starts moving.

Why This Book Exists

Most retirement books are about building wealth. Far fewer explain what happens after that — how savings become income, and how taxes quietly take a cut of every dollar along the way.

This book exists to help you:

• Understand which income sources trigger which taxes, and which ones don't

• Sequence withdrawals so your money is taxed as lightly as the rules allow

• Avoid the traps that catch most retirees off guard — IRMAA surcharges, RMD penalties, surprise Social Security taxation

• Make confident decisions about Roth conversions, charitable giving, and insurance products, without the sales pitch

Every chapter is built to move you from confusion to a plan you can actually run.

Other Books in The Essential Retirement Strategy Series

Practical guides designed to help you make smarter retirement decisions and build long-term financial security.

Available Now

The Essential 401(k) & IRA Retirement Guide

Learn how retirement accounts work, how to maximize contributions, and how to create a smarter withdrawal strategy for long-term financial stability.

The Essential Social Security Retirement Guide

How to maximize your benefits, avoid costly claiming mistakes, and coordinate Social Security with your retirement plan.

The Essential Retirement Tax Strategy Guide

How to reduce taxes on retirement income and build a tax-efficient withdrawal strategy.

The Essential Retirement Income Blueprint

How to turn retirement savings into reliable income streams that last throughout retirement.

Coming Soon

The Essential Medicare Planning Guide

How to select the right Medicare plan for you and protect yourself from unexpected medical expenses.

The Essential Early Retirement Blueprint

Learn how to build a realistic strategy to retire early and learn how to make you money last.

Introduction

Nobody warns you that retirement has its own tax season — and that it can be more confusing than the one you just spent forty years dealing with at work.

Here's the moment it usually hits: you take your first IRA withdrawal, expecting it to feel like cashing in something you already own. Instead, it shows up as ordinary income. Then your Social Security gets taxed too — something you'd half-assumed was off-limits. Then a Medicare premium notice arrives with an extra charge attached, and you find out that's called IRMAA, and that it was triggered by income you didn't think mattered.

None of that is a glitch. It's how the system is built. Taxes don't stop when the paychecks do — they just change shape, and almost nobody explains the new shape in advance.

This book is that explanation. It covers which types of retirement income get taxed and which don't, how to sequence withdrawals across accounts so you're not handing over more than you have to, and how to sidestep the costliest traps: RMD penalties, IRMAA surcharges, and Roth conversions done at the wrong time for the wrong reasons.

You don't need to be wealthy for any of this to matter. A retiree with $400,000 spread across a 401(k), a brokerage account, and Social Security has just as much at stake — sometimes more, because there's less room for error — as someone with several million. The strategies in here aren't exclusive to anyone. They're just rarely explained clearly.

Two things you can count on from here: I won't use a term without explaining it, and the examples are built around real dollar amounts, not vague ranges. Whether you're approaching retirement, already in it, or helping a parent make sense of theirs, the chapters ahead assume you're capable of understanding this — you just haven't had anyone walk you through it yet.

Let's start with the basics: what actually counts as taxable income once the paychecks stop.

Chapter 1: Understanding Retirement Taxes: The Essential Foundations

Chapter at a Glance

What you'll learn in this chapter:

• The five types of retirement income — and which ones the IRS treats completely differently from how you'd expect

• How marginal and effective tax rates actually work, and why "I'm in the 22% bracket" doesn't mean what most people think it means

• The real difference between taxable, tax-deferred, and tax-free accounts — and why holding all three changes your options later

• The deadlines, forms, and recordkeeping habits that keep tax season from turning into a scramble

Estimated reading time: 22 minutes

> ***FIELD NOTE*** *I've sat across from retirees holding a 1099-R for the first time, completely unprepared for the fact that the number on it doesn't match what they thought they'd "earned" that year. That confusion isn't a sign you missed something. It's a sign nobody showed you how this works before now. This chapter fixes that.*

Most people retire with a decent handle on their savings and only a hazy idea of how those savings get taxed. You know roughly what's in your 401(k), your IRA, your brokerage account — but turning those balances into after-tax income, year by year, is a different skill. It's one almost nobody teaches.

That gap shows up fast. A smaller refund than expected. A surprise balance due. Social Security benefits you assumed were tax-free showing up as partially taxable. A Medicare premium that jumped for no obvious reason. None of this is inevitable — it happens because the rules were never explained, not because you did anything wrong.

This chapter lays the foundation: what counts as retirement income, how the federal tax brackets actually work, and which deadlines and forms matter once the regular paycheck stops. Once you can see the structure, the decisions in later chapters — how to sequence withdrawals, when a Roth conversion makes sense, how to avoid an IRMAA surcharge — get a lot easier to make with confidence instead of guesswork.

1.1 How Retirement Income Is Taxed

A paycheck came with one W-2 and one set of rules. Retirement income arrives from several directions at once, each with its own tax treatment. Some of it is taxed as ordinary income. Some gets the lower capital gains rate. Some is tax-free. Some only gets taxed by your state, or not at all. The first job is sorting out which is which.

Five income types cover most retirees:

Earned income — wages, consulting, a small side business — is taxed the same way it always was: ordinary rates, and possibly Social Security and Medicare payroll tax depending on the situation.

Pension income is generally fully taxable as ordinary income when you receive it, reported on Form 1099-R, with one exception: if you contributed after-tax dollars to the plan yourself, a portion of each payment may come back to you tax-free as a return of your own contributions.

Retirement account distributions — traditional IRAs, 401(k)s, 403(b)s — are mostly taxed as ordinary income too. You deferred the tax going in; you pay it coming out. If you ever made nondeductible IRA contributions, part of each withdrawal is a tax-free return of basis, but for most people, the bulk of every distribution is ordinary income.

Social Security is the one that surprises people most. It is not automatically tax-free, and it is not automatically taxed at 85%. The actual figure depends on a calculation called combined income — your adjusted gross income, plus any tax-exempt interest, plus half of your Social Security benefit. Compare that number to thresholds set by your filing status, and the result determines whether 0%, up to 50%, or up to 85% of your benefit gets added to your taxable income.

That last point trips people up constantly: "up to 85% taxable" does not mean an 85% tax rate. It means at most 85 cents of every Social Security dollar gets added to your taxable income, then taxed at your regular marginal rate. The other 15 cents stays tax-free no matter what.

This is where a lot of retirees get caught off guard. Say you pull an extra $20,000 from a traditional IRA one year to cover a home repair. That withdrawal is ordinary income, which raises your combined income, which can push more of your Social Security benefit into taxable territory. One withdrawal decision, two layers of tax. We'll come back to this "tax ripple effect" throughout the book, because managing it is one of the more valuable skills in this entire guide.

Investment income from taxable brokerage or bank accounts — interest, dividends, capital gains — gets taxed annually as it's earned, at either ordinary or capital gains rates depending on the type.

And then there's tax-free income: qualified Roth withdrawals, certain municipal bond interest, some insurance payouts. We'll return to these throughout the book, but the core idea to take away now is simple — "retirement income" isn't one tax category. It's five or six categories wearing the same name.

Ordinary Income vs. Capital Gains

Ordinary rates apply by default: wages, pensions, IRA and 401(k) withdrawals, taxable interest, and short-term gains all fall here, taxed on a progressive scale that climbs as your income rises.

Capital gains rates apply to profits from selling investments in taxable accounts — and only if you held the asset more than a year. Sell sooner, and the gain is taxed at ordinary rates instead. Qualified dividends get the same favorable long-term rate.

This distinction creates real choices. Need $20,000 this year? Pull it from a traditional IRA and it's $20,000 of ordinary income. Pull it from a taxable brokerage account instead, and you might owe tax on only the capital gains portion — often a fraction of that $20,000, taxed at a lower rate. Same dollar amount, very different tax bill, depending entirely on which account it came from.

Capital losses work in your favor too: they offset gains, and within limits, they can offset a small amount of ordinary income as well. Managing gains and losses deliberately — something later chapters cover under tax-efficient withdrawal sequencing — starts with recognizing that not every withdrawn dollar is taxed the same way.

State Taxes

Federal rules apply no matter where you live. State rules don't. Some states tax retirement income exactly like wages. Others exempt Social Security, or pensions, or both. A handful have no income tax at all and lean on sales or property tax instead.

The difference can run into thousands of dollars a year — which is exactly why so many retirees consider relocating. That said, taxes are one variable among several. Cost of living, healthcare access, and proximity to family all matter too, and a no-income-tax state can quietly make it up in property tax. We'll revisit "retirement geography" later in the book. For now, just remember to layer your state's specific rules on top of everything federal you're about to learn.

1.2 Tax Brackets and the Three Account Buckets

Marginal vs. Effective Rate

The U.S. tax system is progressive — picture income filling a series of shelves, each taxed at a different rate. Fill the lowest shelf, spill into the next one, and so on. Crossing into a higher bracket doesn't retroactively raise the rate on everything below it — only the new dollars on the new shelf get the higher rate.

Your marginal rate is the rate on your next dollar. Your effective rate is your total tax divided by your total taxable income — almost always lower than your marginal rate, because of how the brackets stack. Someone whose income reaches the 22% bracket might have an effective rate closer to 12%.

Why does this distinction matter? Because every decision about whether to take an extra IRA distribution, realize a gain, or convert to a Roth comes down to one question: what will I pay on these specific extra dollars? That's your marginal rate talking, not your effective rate.

Three Account Types, Three Tax Treatments

Taxable accounts — ordinary brokerage and bank accounts — get taxed annually on interest, dividends, and realized gains. No required withdrawals, no penalty for tapping them whenever you like.

Tax-deferred accounts — traditional IRAs, 401(k)s, 403(b)s — defer tax until withdrawal, at which point most of the money comes out as ordinary income regardless of how it grew. Once you hit the applicable age, the IRS forces the issue with required minimum distributions, whether you need the cash or not.

Tax-free accounts — Roth IRAs and Roth employer plans — flip the order. You pay tax going in, then qualified withdrawals come out completely tax-free, with no RMDs during your lifetime under current rules.

Holding a mix of all three is what's called tax diversification, and it's the foundation for almost every strategy in the rest of this book — including the bracket-filling techniques we'll cover when we get to withdrawal sequencing.

Three Myths That Cost Retirees Money

"All withdrawals are taxed the same." They're not. $50,000 pulled entirely from a traditional IRA hits your return very differently than $50,000 split across a taxable account, a Roth, and a small IRA withdrawal.

"Roth withdrawals are always tax-free." Only qualified ones — which means meeting both an age requirement and a five-year holding clock. Miss either one, and earnings can be taxed and penalized.

"Always withdraw taxable accounts first, then tax-deferred, then Roth." This default order works often enough that it became conventional wisdom, but it isn't universal. Drawing from a traditional IRA early in a low-income year can fill cheap tax brackets and shrink future RMDs. Realizing gains in a taxable account during a lean year can reset your cost basis. The right order depends on your numbers, not a rule of thumb — which is exactly what Chapter 4 is built to help you figure out.

1.3 Deadlines and Paperwork

Required Minimum Distributions

Tax-deferred accounts come with a deadline attached: once you reach the applicable age, the IRS requires annual withdrawals of at least a minimum amount, calculated from your balance and life expectancy. Miss it, and the penalty is steep — currently 25% of the shortfall, reduced to 10% if corrected promptly. Plan around your RMD schedule rather than discovering it the hard way; we'll dig into RMD strategy in detail in Chapter 4.

Key Forms

Form 1099-R covers distributions from pensions, annuities, IRAs, and employer plans — multiple accounts mean multiple forms, and the IRS matches every one against your return. Form SSA-1099 reports your Social Security benefits and feeds directly into the combined income calculation from earlier in this chapter. Round out the picture with 1099-INT, 1099-DIV, and 1099-B for interest, dividends, and investment sales.

Filing Deadlines

The federal deadline is still April 15th. An extension moves the filing date to October — it does not move the payment date. If you expect to owe, pay by April or face interest charges regardless of any extension. Retirees with multiple income sources and light withholding often need quarterly estimated payments to avoid an underpayment penalty; large IRA distributions or capital gains without any withholding are the most common way people get caught out here.

Keeping Records

Your employer's payroll department used to handle this. Now it's on you. A simple yearly folder — physical or digital — for statements, 1099s, and SSA-1099 forms does most of the work: it speeds up filing, catches the occasional misclassified distribution before it becomes an IRS notice, and gives you the data you'll need for every strategy in the chapters ahead.

Next: the chapters that follow build directly on this foundation. Chapter 2 maps out exactly which moves trigger taxes you didn't see coming.

Key Takeaways

- Retirement income isn't one tax category — earned income, pensions, IRA/401(k) withdrawals, Social Security, investment income, and Roth withdrawals are all taxed differently
- Social Security is taxed on a sliding scale (0%, up to 50%, or up to 85%) based on "combined income" — never an 85% tax rate, just up to 85% of the benefit added to taxable income
- Your marginal rate (tax on your next dollar) and effective rate (tax ÷ total income) are different numbers — decisions about withdrawals and conversions should be based on the marginal rate
- Taxable, tax-deferred, and tax-free accounts each have distinct rules; holding a mix of all three ("tax diversification") is what gives you flexibility later
- RMDs carry a steep penalty for being missed — currently 25% of the shortfall, reduced to 10% if corrected promptly
- The standard withdrawal order ("taxable first, then tax-deferred, then Roth") is a reasonable default, not a universal rule

Chapter 2: Mapping Your Income Sources: Knowing What Triggers Taxes

Chapter at a Glance

What you'll learn in this chapter:

• How "provisional income" decides whether your Social Security gets taxed — and why the math catches almost everyone off guard at least once

• The exact thresholds by filing status where 0%, 50%, and 85% of your benefit becomes taxable

• How 401(k) and IRA withdrawals, pensions, annuities, and investment income each get taxed differently — and why that difference is the whole game

• How to build a one-page "income map" you can actually use

Estimated reading time: 26 minutes

> ***FIELD NOTE*** *The retirees who get the most surprised by Social Security taxation are the ones who did everything else right. They saved diligently, built a healthy IRA, and then got a letter saying 85% of their benefit counted as taxable income. Nobody warned them that being a good saver is exactly what triggers it. This chapter is the warning.*

Retirement income has a way of sneaking up on you. For decades the focus was saving — 401(k)s, IRAs, maybe a pension, Social Security taxes coming out of every paycheck. Then the paycheck stops, and the whole game flips. Instead of accumulation, it's withdrawal: turning a nest egg into something you can actually live on. That's when most retirees discover something unsettling — the IRS is a silent partner in nearly every income source you have, and the rules for each one are different.

This chapter shines a light on those rules. You'll see where your income comes from, how each stream gets taxed, and what actually triggers a bigger bill. Instead of treating "taxes" as one line on a form, you'll start seeing them as a set of levers — levers that move when certain income appears, disappears, or spikes. That awareness is the foundation for everything in the chapters ahead: withdrawal sequencing, Roth conversions, managing Medicare premiums. You can't plan around pieces you can't see.

We'll start with Social Security, since it's usually the first income source retirees turn on and the one everything else gets coordinated around. From there: 401(k) and IRA withdrawals, the workhorses of most retirement portfolios and the biggest drivers of tax swings when mismanaged. Then pensions, annuities, investments, and rental income — what's taxed, what isn't, and how to track the taxable share so nothing catches you off guard at filing time.

As you read, hold one question in the back of your mind: if I add one more dollar from this source, what does it do to the rest of my tax picture? That's the real skill here — not just knowing what's taxed directly, but seeing how one dollar from one source can trigger tax on a completely different source. Social Security is the clearest example of this, so that's where we start.

2.1 Social Security Taxation Rules

Social Security feels simple on the surface — you file, you get a benefit, it shows up in your account. The complication is that those benefits may be partially taxable at the federal level, and what triggers it isn't your benefit amount alone. It's your total income picture, measured through something called provisional income.

Understanding Provisional Income

Provisional income — also called combined income — is the IRS's formula for deciding whether your Social Security is taxable, and how much. It is not the same as your adjusted gross income, and that distinction trips up almost everyone the first time they encounter it.

Provisional income is your AGI excluding Social Security itself, plus any tax-exempt interest (municipal bond income, for instance), plus half of your annual Social Security benefit.

That third piece — half your benefit getting pulled back into the calculation before it's even taxed — is the part nobody expects. And the inclusion of "tax-exempt" interest is its own quiet warning:

income that's never normally taxable can still be the thing that makes your Social Security taxable.

The IRS compares your provisional income against fixed dollar thresholds. Cross one, and part of your benefit becomes taxable. Cross further, and more of it does — up to a cap of 85%.

Thresholds by Filing Status

These thresholds are not indexed to inflation, which means they stay fixed while benefits and other income keep growing — quietly pulling more retirees into taxation every year that passes.

For single filers, heads of household, and qualifying widows or widowers:

• Provisional income of $25,000 or less: none of your benefit is taxable

• Between $25,001 and $34,000: up to 50% may be taxable

• Above $34,000: up to 85% may be taxable

For married couples filing jointly:

• $32,000 or less: none taxable

• $32,001 to $44,000: up to 50% taxable

• Above $44,000: up to 85% taxable

"Up to" doesn't mean you're automatically taxed on exactly half or 85% the moment you cross a line — the IRS uses a stepwise calculation that phases in gradually. But from a planning standpoint, treat these thresholds like cliffs anyway. A seemingly modest bump in other income — a bigger IRA withdrawal, a sizable capital gain, a one-time pension payout — can push you across one and pull a meaningfully larger share of your benefit into the taxable column.

Don't think of these thresholds as Social-Security-specific tax brackets. Think of them as tripwires. Cross one, and actions in your other accounts get a multiplier effect — not just taxing that income, but also dragging more of your benefit into the taxable pile alongside it.

Calculating Your Taxable Social Security

The IRS provides a detailed worksheet in Publication 915, and it's more thorough than it needs to be for a quick gut-check. Here's the simplified version:

• Start with your total Social Security benefit for the year (from Form SSA-1099)

• Take half of that

• Add your other income — IRA and 401(k) withdrawals, pensions, interest, dividends, rental income, capital gains

• Add any tax-exempt interest

• That total is your provisional income

• Compare it to your filing-status thresholds above

• The worksheet then tells you the exact taxable percentage, between 0% and 85%

Your tax software or preparer will run the actual math. But running a rough version yourself a couple of times is worth the ten minutes — it's the fastest way to see how an extra $1,000 IRA withdrawal can quietly drag several hundred dollars of your Social Security from nontaxable into taxable, on top of the tax on the withdrawal itself. That's an effective marginal rate well above what the tax table alone would suggest.

Strategies to Manage Social Security Taxation

Once you understand provisional income, you can manage it. The goal isn't necessarily zero tax on your benefit — for some people that's achievable, for most it isn't — it's avoiding the avoidable spikes.

Plan your traditional account distributions deliberately. Withdrawals from 401(k)s and traditional IRAs count fully toward AGI, making them the single biggest lever on provisional income. In years you don't need much, limit withdrawals to what living expenses or your target bracket require. In other years — particularly before Social Security starts or before RMDs kick in — you might intentionally take larger withdrawals to "fill up" a low bracket while it's still available, shrinking the size of the forced withdrawals waiting for you later.

Use Roth accounts as your flexible tool. Qualified Roth withdrawals don't count as taxable income and never enter the provisional income formula at all. That makes Roth money especially valuable for funding a one-time expense — home repairs, a car, a family trip — without triggering extra tax on your Social Security in the process.

Time Roth conversions around your Social Security claiming date. Converting traditional money to Roth creates taxable income in the conversion year, which raises provisional income if you're already collecting benefits. Most retirees find it more efficient to do the bulk of their conversions in the "bridge years" — after work ends but before Social Security starts — specifically to dodge that double hit.

Watch for income spikes. Selling a rental property, realizing a large gain, taking a lump-sum pension buyout, or converting a large IRA balance all in one year can send provisional income soaring. Where possible, spread these events across multiple years instead — staged sales, installment payments, partitioned conversions — to keep more of your benefit in the nontaxable or 50% zone rather than jumping straight to 85%.

This isn't a once-and-done calculation. It's a yearly exercise that connects directly to withdrawal sequencing, Medicare premium thresholds, and legacy planning — all covered in later chapters. Mapping where you stand now, and where you're heading over the next five to ten years, gives you room to adjust while the stakes are still manageable.

2.2 Taxation of 401(k) and IRA Withdrawals

Traditional employer plans and IRAs are usually the single largest pool of retirement wealth, and tax-wise, the rule is simple: money goes in pre-tax, grows tax-deferred, comes out as ordinary income. The complexity isn't the rule — it's how easily these withdrawals push you into higher brackets, trigger more Social Security taxation, and raise other income-sensitive costs along the way.

Ordinary Income Treatment

Withdrawals from traditional 401(k)s, 403(b)s, 457 plans, and traditional IRAs are taxed as ordinary income — every dollar (except any nondeductible-contribution basis tracked on Form 8606) gets added to your taxable income for the year, stacking on top of wages, pensions, or anything else. There's no preferential rate the way there is for long-term capital gains.

Because the system is progressive, a large distribution can land partly in a lower bracket and partly in a higher one. And as discussed above, the same withdrawal can simultaneously raise your provisional income and pull more Social Security into taxable territory. When mapping your income, ask: if I need $X this year, how much should come from traditional accounts versus other sources? Could taxable or Roth accounts cover part of it instead, keeping traditional withdrawals at a level that stays in a comfortable bracket? This kind of simple annual planning — often done late in the year once you can see your full picture — can save thousands over the course of retirement.

Required Minimum Distributions

Eventually, the government stops waiting. RMDs mark that point. Under current law, the starting age depends on your birth year — 73 for many current retirees, 75 for those born in 1960 or later. Employer plans sometimes allow non-5%-owners to delay RMDs from a current employer's plan past that age, subject to plan rules, so it's worth confirming the exact starting date for each account you hold.

The calculation is your prior year-end balance divided by an IRS life expectancy factor, recalculated every year. You can always take more than the RMD; you cannot take less without a penalty on the shortfall.

That penalty used to run as high as 50% of the missed amount. Recent changes have reduced it in many cases, but it remains steep, and it stacks on top of the ordinary tax owed once you correct the error — it doesn't replace it. Missing an RMD is one of the most expensive avoidable mistakes in retirement tax planning.

RMDs raise your taxable income whether you need the cash or not. If you have other income — a pension, rental income, ongoing work — your RMD might exceed your actual spending needs. You still have to take it and report it, but you can reinvest the after-tax amount, gift it, or send it directly to charity as a Qualified Charitable Distribution (QCD), which we'll cover in more depth in Chapter 9.

Think of RMDs as forced income: a baseline of taxable income in later retirement that you can't easily reduce after the fact. That's exactly why it's worth starting controlled withdrawals or Roth conversions in your sixties if your traditional balances are large relative to what you actually spend — shrinking the size of the RMD problem before it arrives, rather than being surprised by it later.

Early Withdrawal Penalties and Exceptions

Some readers will need funds before age 59½. Withdrawals from traditional accounts before that age generally face two layers of cost: ordinary income tax plus a 10% early withdrawal penalty. Exceptions exist — disability, certain medical expenses, some education costs, first-time home purchases from an IRA, substantially equal periodic payments under Section 72(t), and a handful of newer emergency-withdrawal provisions if your plan allows them. Even when the penalty doesn't apply, the withdrawal is still ordinary taxable income, feeding into AGI and potentially into provisional income if you're already collecting Social Security.

If you're planning to retire in your late fifties, map out which accounts you can tap without penalty — taxable investments, Roth contributions (though not earnings, unless qualified), or an employer plan offering penalty-free withdrawals for separated employees at 55 or later. The question isn't just "can I access this money" — it's what the tax and penalty cost does to your broader income map.

Withdrawal Sequencing as a Tax Tool

Deciding which accounts to draw from, and when, is where everything in this chapter pays off. Coordinating withdrawals across taxable, tax-deferred, and tax-free accounts can meaningfully reduce your lifetime tax bill and smooth your tax profile year to year — we'll build a full framework for this in Chapter 4, but the foundation starts here.

A common early-retirement approach, before RMDs and sometimes before Social Security, blends sources: modest traditional withdrawals up to a chosen bracket, supplemented by taxable-account withdrawals (which may include some capital gains, but at lower rates), with Roth held in reserve. Because long-term capital gains can sometimes be taxed at 0% for retirees in lower brackets, there's real opportunity to harvest gains at little or no cost if traditional withdrawals are managed carefully alongside them.

As Social Security and RMDs enter the picture, the balance shifts. More of your income becomes fixed and unavoidable, so you may scale back additional traditional withdrawals to avoid bracket creep and rising provisional income. Roth and taxable accounts become the flexible valves you open or close to adjust spending without adding to ordinary income.

Sequencing also touches Medicare. Income-Related Monthly Adjustment Amounts (IRMAA) for Part B and Part D are based on a modified AGI measure — large traditional withdrawals or big gains in one year can mean higher premiums two years later. Every income source has ripple effects, and seeing them together is what lets you spot a decision that looks fine this year but costs you down the line.

2.3 Taxed and Untaxed Investment and Pension Income

Beyond Social Security and retirement accounts, many retirees lean on pensions, annuities, investment portfolios, and rental properties. Run each one through the same three questions: Is this ordinary income or capital gain? Is any part a return of my own after-tax money? Does it create hidden income for provisional income or Medicare purposes? — and the picture gets a lot clearer.

Pension Income

Traditional defined-benefit pensions are, in most cases, fully taxable as ordinary income, treated much like a traditional IRA distribution. If your pension was funded entirely with pre-tax employer dollars, every payment is taxable. If you made after-tax contributions yourself, part of each payment may come back tax-free as a return of basis — your 1099-R will typically show the breakdown, and keeping records of any after-tax contributions protects you from being taxed twice on the same money.

State treatment varies widely — some states tax pensions fully, some exempt certain types (public or military pensions, for example), some have no income tax at all. Worth distinguishing federal from state exposure here, especially if relocation is on the table.

Annuity Income

Annuities are insurance contracts that can provide guaranteed retirement income, and their tax treatment depends on whether they're qualified (funded with pre-tax money inside an IRA or employer plan) or non-qualified (purchased with after-tax dollars in a taxable account).

Qualified annuity distributions are generally fully taxable as ordinary income, just like a traditional IRA — there's no basis to recover tax-free, because the money was never taxed going in.

Non-qualified annuities mix principal and earnings. The principal is after-tax money; earnings grow tax-deferred inside the contract. Payments use an "exclusion ratio" to split each one into taxable earnings and nontaxable return of principal. Once your basis is fully recovered, every later payment becomes fully taxable.

For mapping purposes: the taxable portion counts as ordinary income and feeds into AGI and provisional income; the nontaxable return-of-principal portion doesn't. That distinction matters if you're weighing whether to annuitize a contract, take withdrawals, or exchange one annuity for another.

Investment Income

Interest from bank accounts, corporate bonds, and most bond funds is taxed as ordinary income and flows straight into AGI and provisional income. Municipal bond interest may be exempt from federal tax, but — as we covered earlier — it still counts toward provisional income for Social Security purposes. "Tax-free" doesn't mean invisible to the formulas that actually matter.

Dividends come in two flavors. Qualified dividends, from many U.S. corporations and held for a minimum period, are taxed at the same preferential rates as long-term capital gains — 0%, 15%, or 20% depending on your income. Ordinary dividends are taxed as regular income. For many retirees with modest total income, qualified dividends and long-term gains can land in the 0% bracket entirely, which creates real planning opportunities to harvest gains or dividends at little to no tax cost.

Capital gains are realized when you sell for more than your cost basis. Long-term gains (held over a year) get preferential rates; short-term gains are taxed as ordinary income. Because you control the timing of most sales, this is a genuine planning lever — harvest more in low-income years, defer in high-income ones.

All of this — interest, dividends, gains — feeds AGI, and from there, provisional income and potentially IRMAA. When you map your income, look not just at portfolio size but at its tax character: how much is likely to show up as ordinary income versus preferentially taxed gains, and how much flexibility you have to time it.

Rental and Other Passive Income

Rental income is generally taxable, but the tax code allows you to deduct property taxes, insurance, maintenance, management fees, mortgage interest, and — importantly — depreciation before arriving at taxable income. Depreciation is a non-cash expense that spreads the cost of the building (not the land) over a set number of years, which can reduce or eliminate taxable rental income even on a cash-flow-positive property. When you eventually sell, some or all of that depreciation gets "recaptured" and taxed, often at a higher rate than your long-term capital gain on the rest of the profit. Depreciation doesn't make income disappear — it shifts it to a later year.

Rental losses are subject to passive activity loss rules: sometimes usable against other income, sometimes suspended and carried forward against future rental income or sale gains. Rental income is rarely as simple as rent minus bills — you need to track both the annual picture and the longer-term buildup of suspended losses and depreciation that will affect your taxes when you sell. Depending on your involvement, rental or side-business income may also trigger self-employment tax, which is one more reason to coordinate planning across every income source, not just the obvious ones.

Building Your Income Map

Retirement income isn't a single stream — it's a network of rivers and tributaries, each with its own rules and hidden currents. Social Security may or may not be taxable depending on provisional income. Traditional 401(k) and IRA withdrawals are always ordinary income and can trigger more Social Security taxation and higher Medicare costs along with it. Pensions and annuities add to the ordinary income column, with some contracts returning principal tax-free. Investments spill out interest, dividends, and gains, some preferential, some not. Rental income weaves in its own mix of deductions, depreciation, and potential recapture.

Mapping your income means identifying each flow, labeling its tax character, and watching how they interact at different income levels. It's not just "what will I receive" — it's "which dollars get taxed when, and what do they trigger elsewhere."

Your action step: list your expected income sources — Social Security, pensions, retirement accounts, investments, rentals, any continued work — and mark next to each whether it's ordinary income, capital gain/dividend rate, partially tax-free, or untaxed. Then mark which ones you control (voluntary withdrawals, asset sales) and which are fixed (RMDs, pension payments). That map is the foundation for everything from here forward — turning "knowing what triggers taxes" into actually keeping more of what you've saved.

Key Takeaways

• "Provisional income" — AGI, plus tax-exempt interest, plus half your Social Security benefit — determines how much of your benefit is taxable

• Provisional income thresholds are not indexed to inflation, so more retirees get pulled into taxation every year that passes

• A single extra withdrawal can have a "double effect": taxed itself, and simultaneously pulling more Social Security into the taxable column

• RMD age depends on birth year — 73 for many current retirees, 75 for those born in 1960 or later

• Early withdrawals before 59½ generally face ordinary tax plus a 10% penalty, with specific exceptions (disability, medical expenses, first-time home purchase, and others)

• Build a simple income map: list every source, label its tax character, and mark which ones you control versus which are fixed

Chapter 3: Tax Traps to Avoid: Common Mistakes That Erode Savings

Chapter at a Glance

What you'll learn in this chapter:

• The RMD mistakes that cost the most money — and why most of them are created a decade before the first missed deadline

• How Qualified Charitable Distributions can turn a forced RMD into a tax-free act of giving

• Why stacking income sources in the same year is the single biggest unforced error retirees make

• How IRMAA's two-year lookback creates a trap that springs long after the decision that caused it

Estimated reading time: 28 minutes

> ***FIELD NOTE*** *Almost nobody loses money in retirement from one reckless decision. They lose it from three or four perfectly reasonable choices made without looking at each other — claiming Social Security here, converting an IRA there, selling an investment somewhere else. None of it looks like a mistake in the moment. This chapter is about learning to see the whole board instead of one square at a time.*

Most people picture retirement in terms of time and lifestyle — sleeping past the alarm, traveling on your own schedule, spoiling grandchildren. Almost nobody pictures it in terms of tax brackets, Medicare surcharges, and IRS deadlines. But those behind-the-scenes details quietly shape what retirement actually feels like, because they determine how much of your money you get to keep.

This chapter zooms in on what can erode the income you've built: the tax traps that surprise even careful savers. These aren't exotic loopholes — they're everyday mistakes. Missing an RMD. Stacking too much income into one year. Triggering a Medicare surcharge you didn't see coming. Individually small, repeated over a 20- or 30-year retirement, they cost real money.

The goal isn't to turn you into a tax professional — it's to give you enough clarity to see the traps coming and route around them. Notice the recurring themes as you read: timing, coordination, and planning several years out instead of one return at a time.

3.1 Required Minimum Distribution Pitfalls

RMDs are one of the most misunderstood features of the retirement tax landscape. During your working years, "put as much as you can into tax-deferred accounts" is uncontroversial advice. The problem shows up decades later, when the IRS finally says it's time to take some back — and pay tax when you do.

Understanding the Requirement

Most traditional IRAs, traditional 401(k)s, 403(b)s, 457(b)s, SEPs, and SIMPLE IRAs fall under RMD rules. Starting at a specified age — 72 under older rules for many retirees, later under newer law — you must withdraw at least a minimum amount each year, generally your December 31 balance divided by an IRS life-expectancy factor. Your custodian often computes this for you, but the legal responsibility sits with you, not the institution.

The penalty for missing it is still serious, even though current law is more forgiving than the old 50% rule. Today the excise tax generally runs 25% of the shortfall, reduced to 10% if corrected within the applicable window. Say your RMD is $20,000 and you simply forget. The excise tax could run $5,000 — or $2,000 if corrected quickly — on top of the ordinary income tax due once you finally take the distribution. The penalty doesn't replace the tax. It stacks on top of it.

The trap isn't only forgetting outright. It can come from misjudging your very first RMD deadline. Some rules let you delay your first RMD until April 1 of the year after you reach the required age — which sounds like a reprieve but can actually create a worse problem: two RMDs landing in the same calendar year, potentially doubling that year's taxable income and pushing you into a higher bracket. Know exactly when your RMDs begin, how they're calculated, and what delaying actually costs. A standing distribution instruction with your custodian is the simplest insurance against a penalty that serves no purpose except enriching the Treasury at your expense.

Planning for RMD Tax Impact

Even when you take RMDs on time, the way they interact with everything else can cause a second layer of trouble. RMDs are ordinary income, stacking on top of pensions, wages, consulting income, rental income, and up to 85% of Social Security if your combined income is high enough. This stacking effect can push you into higher brackets, increase how much of your Social Security is taxed, and trigger surtaxes like the Net Investment Income Tax or Medicare surcharges.

A familiar pattern: a couple retires in their early sixties, lives comfortably off savings and maybe a pension, and leaves their IRAs untouched. The accounts keep compounding. By the time RMDs begin, those IRAs have doubled or more. The couple starts Social Security around the same time. Suddenly, in their early-to-mid seventies, RMDs plus pension plus benefits push them into a higher bracket than they ever saw while working. The surprise isn't that the money is taxable — that was always the deal — it's how little flexibility they have left to control the timing.

Planning ahead is the antidote. The years between retirement and the start of RMDs are often unusually low-tax years, and they're the best window for strategic withdrawals or Roth conversions from traditional accounts. Deliberately filling up lower brackets with controlled withdrawals shrinks future balances — and therefore future RMDs. The goal isn't avoiding tax completely. It's smoothing it over many years instead of facing a sudden spike later.

Roth conversions deserve special mention here. You pay tax now on the converted amount, but future growth is tax-free, and Roth IRAs carry no RMDs under current law. Conversions done in modest, planned amounts — rather than one large conversion in a single high-income year — shrink future RMDs while keeping more flexibility intact. We'll build out the full conversion strategy in Chapter 5; the principle to take from here is that RMD problems are usually created in the decade before they begin, not the year the first required-distribution notice arrives.

Avoiding the "Catch-Up" Mentality

There's a subtler, behavioral RMD trap. Many retirees treat the RMD as an annoying chore to put off until December. Understandable — nobody enjoys watching a balance drop — but waiting and pulling a large lump sum at year-end creates unnecessary tax and cash-flow consequences. A large single withdrawal can push a chunk of income into a higher bracket than the same total spread across the year would. And tax law doesn't allow "catching up" later if you forget — the RMD is fixed to that year's starting balance, and the penalty applies to whatever you failed to distribute on time.

A better habit: set up monthly or quarterly distributions that, in total, satisfy your annual RMD. This spreads the taxable income evenly, keeps estimated payments and withholding more predictable, and matches how most households actually manage cash flow — bills don't arrive only in December. It also has an investment angle: in a volatile market, smaller distributions throughout the year reduce the risk of being forced to sell a large chunk of your portfolio at a particularly bad moment.

Using Charitable Giving to Offset RMDs

For charitably inclined retirees, there's a trap and an opportunity wrapped together here. The trap is giving in a way that produces little or no tax benefit. The opportunity is the Qualified Charitable Distribution (QCD) — a rule that lets you, once you're old enough (currently age 70½), transfer money directly from your IRA to a qualified charity. Done correctly, the amount sent counts toward your RMD but is excluded from your taxable income entirely.

That's meaningfully different from taking the RMD into your checking account and then writing a check to the charity yourself — in that version, the full distribution is taxable, and your deduction depends on whether you itemize. With a QCD, you never recognize the income in the first place.

The cascading benefit is real: because a QCD reduces your AGI, it can help keep you out of a higher bracket, reduce the taxable share of your Social Security, and lower your exposure to IRMAA and NIIT. In a year when you're already close to one of those thresholds, using a QCD instead of a taxable RMD can be the difference between staying under the line and crossing it.

Get the mechanics right: the money has to move directly from your IRA custodian to the charity — if it touches your personal account first, it loses QCD status. Keep documentation from both the charity and your custodian. Not every account qualifies, and donor-advised funds are not eligible recipients under current rules. If you're charitably inclined and subject to RMDs, this single rule can turn an unavoidable tax event into a tax-efficient act of generosity.

3.2 Stacking Income and Bracket Creep

Even with RMDs well managed, a second category of traps comes from how different income sources pile on top of each other. Most retirees shift from one paycheck to a mix: Social Security, a pension, part-time work, traditional IRA withdrawals, Roth distributions, investment income, maybe annuity payments. Each one looks harmless alone. Together, at the wrong moment, they can shove you into a higher bracket, increase the taxable share of Social Security, and trigger surtaxes — all at once.

How Combined Income Compounds

Tax brackets are progressive — only the dollars in each bracket get taxed at that bracket's rate — but as income stacks, more of it spills into higher brackets. This is where the difference between marginal rate (the rate on your next dollar) and effective rate (your total tax divided by total income) becomes important. Misunderstanding it leads people either to fear any increase in income, or to ignore how close they actually are to a bracket boundary.

In retirement, combined income carries an extra wrinkle: the Social Security "provisional income" measure includes half your benefit plus other taxable income and certain tax-exempt interest. Once that crosses specific thresholds, up to 50% and then up to 85% of your benefit can become taxable — meaning a modest extra IRA withdrawal can have a double effect, taxed itself and simultaneously pulling more of your benefit into taxable territory.

Investment income plays into this too. Dividends, interest, and capital gains stack on top of pensions, RMDs, and earned income. Sell investments with large embedded gains in the same year you take a big RMD or do a Roth conversion, and the combination can bump you into a higher bracket and trigger NIIT or IRMAA. The surprise usually isn't that any single source is unusual — it's that nobody stepped back to see the full picture before the year was locked in.

Sequencing Withdrawals to Manage the Stack

There's no universal sequencing rule, but one common starting framework: taxable accounts first, tax-deferred next, Roth last. The logic is that taxable withdrawals are often part return-of-principal and part long-term capital gain (taxed favorably), while tax-deferred and Roth accounts keep compounding untouched.

Strict adherence to that pattern, though, can recreate the exact RMD problem from earlier in this chapter — letting tax-deferred accounts grow so large that future mandatory withdrawals become painful. A more nuanced approach blends sources to manage brackets and surtaxes across many years, not just minimize this year's bill. You might fund a baseline from taxable accounts in your sixties while also taking modest voluntary withdrawals or conversions from traditional IRAs, gradually shrinking them before RMDs begin.

Delaying Social Security plays into this too. Waiting increases your eventual monthly check, and the resulting low-income years early in retirement are often ideal for Roth conversions or strategic taxable withdrawals. Once benefits start and become partly taxable, leaning more on Roth withdrawals helps avoid pushing more of that benefit into taxable territory.

Using Bracket Awareness Deliberately

Knowing your current marginal bracket — and how much room remains before the next one — is one of the most useful planning habits in this entire book. You don't need to memorize tax tables, just have a working sense of your projected taxable income and where it lands. From there you can ask real questions: if I withdraw an extra $10,000 from my IRA this year, what bracket do those dollars land in? Do I have headroom for a Roth conversion without spilling into the next bracket?

"Filling the bracket" is the practical version of this: if you're comfortably within a bracket with headroom before the next threshold, you might intentionally take an additional IRA withdrawal or partial conversion to use that headroom — taxed at a known, controlled rate you've decided is acceptable given what you expect rates to look like later. This isn't a one-time calculation. Treat it as an annual, maybe even quarterly, habit: estimate income, see where you sit, decide whether to accelerate or defer.

Don't forget state brackets. Federal rules get the attention, but state systems can swing your net income significantly — some tax retirement income fully, some exempt Social Security or certain pensions, some have no income tax but make it up with property or sales tax. "No income tax" sounds attractive until you check what it's compensating for. If a move is on the horizon, the timing of withdrawals relative to that move is its own planning lever.

3.3 Unexpected Medicare and Surtax Surprises

Once you enroll in Medicare at 65, your tax picture gains new moving parts. Many retirees assume Medicare makes healthcare costs predictable. In reality, premiums vary significantly for higher earners, and surtaxes like NIIT can skim a portion of investment returns once income crosses certain lines. The common thread: a one-year income spike — often intentional, like a Roth conversion or asset sale — can have consequences you don't see until years later.

Understanding IRMAA

Medicare Part B and Part D premiums are income-based. Most people pay the standard amount; higher earners pay that plus an Income-Related Monthly Adjustment Amount, or IRMAA. IRMAA is calculated from your modified AGI — but from your tax return two years prior. That two-year lookback is exactly where the trap lies.

Do a large Roth conversion, sell a rental property with a big gain, or take an unusually large IRA distribution to buy a vacation home, and in the year you do it, you may have fully accepted the higher tax as a deliberate trade-off. Two years later, your Medicare premium jumps for an entire calendar year, and the connection to that earlier decision feels distant and frustrating — especially if your income has already dropped back down.

Even moderate income increases can push you into a higher IRMAA tier, adding hundreds of dollars a month. The goal isn't avoiding income altogether — sometimes a large withdrawal or conversion is genuinely worth it — it's choosing the size and timing with full awareness of what arrives two years later.

Net Investment Income Tax Basics

NIIT is a 3.8% surtax on certain net investment income once your modified AGI exceeds specific thresholds — commonly $200,000 for individuals, $250,000 for married couples filing jointly. It applies to interest, dividends, capital gains, rental income, and other passive sources. It doesn't apply directly to most retirement account distributions, but because those distributions raise your modified AGI, they can push you over the threshold and expose more of your investment income to the extra tax.

RMDs play a role here too — a large required distribution can push income high enough to trip NIIT, particularly alongside substantial taxable-account earnings. A retiree who thinks of themselves as solidly "middle income" can discover, in a year they sell a long-held property or a concentrated stock position, that the gain is hit with both capital gains tax and NIIT on top.

You don't need to memorize NIIT's mechanics, but be aware that above certain income levels, investment returns aren't taxed solely at the familiar capital gains or dividend rates. Holding an investment a few extra weeks to qualify for long-term treatment, or spreading sales across multiple years, can help you stay below the threshold or at least limit how much income gets exposed to it.

Coordinating Income to Control Surtax Exposure

Controlling IRMAA and NIIT exposure is less about eliminating specific income types and more about timing when they land. Just as you can "fill" a tax bracket without spilling over, you can fill your IRMAA or NIIT headroom. If you're already near an IRMAA threshold in a given year because of RMDs and other fixed income, it may make sense to push discretionary income events — a Roth conversion, a large gain realization — into a different year with more room.

Conversely, if a high-income year is unavoidable — a business or property sale, for instance — it can make sense to consolidate other planned transactions into that same year, accepting one IRMAA and NIIT hit rather than spreading smaller hits across multiple years that, added up, cost more in cumulative surcharges. Surtaxes aren't random — they arise from predictable combinations of income sources you can plan around once you see them coming.

Adjusting When Income Changes

Because IRMAA uses a two-year lookback, there's often a lag between a real income drop and a premium adjustment. If your income falls significantly — the death of a spouse, ending a part-time job, the end of a Roth conversion series — your premium won't automatically catch up. There is a formal appeal process based on Social Security's "life-changing events": marriage, divorce, death of a spouse, work stoppage, or loss of income-producing property, among others. Filing one requires documentation — tax returns, employer or plan statements, a clear explanation of the change — but many retirees don't know the option exists and simply accept a premium that no longer matches their real income.

An annual income review is worth building into your routine — not just for the current year, but projecting two or three years out, asking how planned RMDs, sales, or conversions will land on both your tax return and your Medicare premium. Retirement tax traps rarely come from one reckless decision. They come from reasonable choices made in isolation, without anyone stepping back to see how they interact.

Understanding RMD mechanics, how income stacks across brackets, and the ripple effects of Medicare and investment surtaxes puts you in a position to make deliberate, confident choices instead of getting blindsided two years after the fact.

Key Takeaways

- Most expensive retirement tax mistakes are created a decade before they show up — not in the year the RMD notice arrives
- A Qualified Charitable Distribution (QCD) lets you satisfy your RMD while excluding the amount from taxable income entirely — a real act of tax-efficient giving once you're 70½
- IRMAA is based on income from two years prior — a decision made today can raise your Medicare premium two years from now
- IRMAA and NIIT work on a "cliff" basis in places — crossing a threshold by even a small amount can trigger a meaningful increase
- The Net Investment Income Tax (NIIT) is a 3.8% surtax above $200,000 (individual) / $250,000 (joint) modified AGI, and applies to interest, dividends, gains, and rental income
- If your income drops because of a "life-changing event" (death of a spouse, divorce, work stoppage), you can request an IRMAA reconsideration rather than wait for the two-year lookback to catch up

Chapter 4: Smart Withdrawal Sequencing: Stretching Your Nest Egg with Taxes in Mind

Chapter at a Glance

What you'll learn in this chapter:

• The three-bucket framework — taxable, tax-deferred, Roth — and the order that usually (not always) makes sense

• When the "conventional wisdom" withdrawal order actively backfires, and how to spot it

• How to coordinate withdrawals with Social Security timing, RMDs, and Medicare thresholds as one connected system

• Tax-loss harvesting and the wash sale rule — turning market dips into tax assets

Estimated reading time: 30 minutes

> ***FIELD NOTE*** *Two retirees can have the exact same account balances and end up with very different lifetime tax bills, just because one of them thought about withdrawal order and the other didn't. This is the highest-leverage chapter in the book — not because the ideas are complicated, but because almost nobody applies them on purpose.*

Most people think of retirement planning as a question of "do I have enough?" Once you actually reach the doorstep of retirement, a second question becomes just as important: how do I spend what I've saved without giving too much of it away in taxes? Taxes can quietly become one of the largest expenses in retirement, especially with savings spread across taxable brokerage accounts, traditional IRAs and 401(k)s, and Roth accounts. The order you tap these accounts, and how you coordinate them year to year, can add years to your portfolio's life — or, handled poorly, shorten it considerably.

This chapter turns your nest egg into a tax-aware income system. Instead of "I'll pull from whatever account is convenient," you start asking: if I take this dollar from here instead of there, what does that do to my tax bill this year — and ten years from now? Two retirees with identical balances can end up with very different outcomes simply because one used a more thoughtful withdrawal order.

4.1 Order of Withdrawal: Getting the Sequence Working for You

Picture your retirement savings as three buckets, each with its own tax rules. Taxable accounts generate interest, dividends, and gains taxed along the way. Traditional IRAs and 401(k)s defer tax until withdrawal. Roth accounts require tax upfront, then deliver tax-free growth and tax-free qualified withdrawals. How you sequence these buckets influences not just this year's tax bill, but your lifetime taxes and how long your portfolio lasts.

Traditional advice says: taxable first, tax-deferred next, Roth last. Research generally supports this as a baseline, because taxable accounts tend to be the least tax-efficient place to hold investments over long periods, while tax-deferred and Roth accounts compound more powerfully. Studies of withdrawal sequencing show that leading with taxable money can let a portfolio last several years longer than reversing the order. But like any rule of thumb, it has real exceptions — the rest of this section covers the classic sequence, then how to adapt it.

Taxable Accounts First: Flexibility and Control

Starting here usually offers the most flexibility. Selling investments in a taxable account may trigger capital gains tax, but you control when and how those gains get realized. Sell low-gain holdings and the impact is modest; hold over a year and you get long-term rates, often well below ordinary income rates. Some retirees with low taxable income even land in the 0% capital gains bracket entirely.

Taxable withdrawals also don't trigger RMDs — take as much or as little as you like, whenever you like. That makes them a flexible bridge in the early retirement years, between your last paycheck and the start of Social Security or RMDs, letting traditional and Roth accounts keep compounding untouched. You can also choose which specific lots to sell — spending down cash and short-term holdings first, trimming appreciated shares in years when other income is low.

Leaning on taxable accounts early also keeps ordinary income lower, which sets up other moves: partial Roth conversions or modest IRA withdrawals at very low marginal rates. Retirees in the 0% capital gains bracket may want to meet spending from taxable accounts while simultaneously filling that bracket with realized gains or repositioning trades, at little to no tax cost.

The limit: relying on taxable accounts exclusively for too long, while leaving large pre-tax balances untouched, sets up exactly the RMD problem covered in Chapter 3 — forced, large, and highly taxable withdrawals later. Taxable-first is a strong starting point, rarely the whole strategy.

Tax-Deferred Accounts Next: Mindful of RMDs and Brackets

Every dollar withdrawn from a traditional IRA or 401(k) generally shows up as ordinary income. Empty these too quickly early on and you risk pushing into higher brackets, increasing the taxable share of Social Security, and triggering Medicare surcharges. Ignore them too long, and RMDs starting in your early seventies will force withdrawals based on IRS formulas regardless of what you actually need.

A thoughtful sequence usually brings tax-deferred withdrawals into the picture before RMDs begin, even while taxable accounts cover most spending — "pre-RMD smoothing." In the years after work ends but before Social Security and RMDs fully ramp up, ordinary income is often unusually low. That's the window to deliberately withdraw modest amounts — enough to fill lower brackets — avoiding much higher marginal rates later once RMDs and other income stack together.

Treat each year as a bracket-management exercise. Decide you're comfortable filling the 12% or 22% bracket but not crossing into the next one, then structure traditional withdrawals to land just under that threshold, covering any additional spending from taxable or Roth sources instead. This smooths your tax profile across retirement and shrinks future RMDs — reducing the risk of large forced withdrawals in your eighties.

This is also where strategic Roth conversions happen — pulling future taxable income into the present, paying tax now on the converted amount, in exchange for tax-free future growth and (for Roth IRAs) no RMDs at all. For many households, the gap years between retirement and RMD age are the single most tax-efficient window for this move, as long as you watch how conversions interact with Social Security taxation, Medicare thresholds, and any means-tested credits.

Roth Accounts Last: Tax-Free Growth and Withdrawals

Roth IRAs and Roth 401(k)s are the crown jewels of the toolkit. Once you satisfy the age and holding-period rules, qualified withdrawals are tax-free, and Roth IRAs escape RMDs entirely during the original owner's lifetime — leave them untouched as long as you like.

Because Roth withdrawals don't count as taxable income, they're ideal for covering a large unplanned expense — a home repair, helping with a grandchild's wedding, a bucket-list trip — without increasing the taxation of Social Security or crossing a Medicare threshold. That's why many advisors suggest preserving Roth money for as long as possible: it functions as a flexible, tax-free reserve.

There's an estate angle too. Beneficiaries inheriting a Roth IRA generally get tax-free withdrawals, even though current rules require emptying the account within a fixed period. Compare that to a traditional account, where heirs owe ordinary income tax on every withdrawal — Roth inheritances are often the more attractive option, which is one more reason to spend down taxable and traditional assets first while letting Roth money keep compounding.

This isn't an absolute rule. In a year with unusually high medical expenses creating large deductions, traditional withdrawals might make more sense, preserving Roth for later. In a year where you want to avoid any increase in taxable income at all, Roth is exactly the source to use. The general pattern holds: every year Roth money stays untouched is another year of tax-free growth.

Hybrid Approaches

In practice, very few retirees follow a strict drain-one-bucket-then-move-on rule. A hybrid approach – pulling from multiple account types in a coordinated way – usually works better, especially with substantial pre-tax balances, expected Social Security or pension income, and both lifestyle and legacy goals in play.

One common hybrid: start with taxable withdrawals, but layer in modest controlled distributions or conversions from traditional accounts early on, even when not strictly needed for spending, specifically to avoid leaving a tax-deferred balance large enough to generate an oversized RMD later. There's no fixed recipe – you revisit the sequence annually based on your tax situation, market performance, and changing needs.

Social Security timing creates another hybrid scenario. If you're delaying benefits to increase your eventual check, the bridge years might lean more heavily on taxable and traditional accounts, targeting withdrawals to roughly match the benefit you're delaying. Once benefits start, you may tilt toward Roth and taxable to avoid pushing more of that benefit into taxable territory.

Estate planning matters here too. If your heirs are in higher brackets than you, spending more aggressively from traditional accounts during your lifetime – locking in tax at your lower rate – and leaving Roth or appreciated taxable assets for them can make sense. If your primary beneficiary is a charity, which owes no tax on inherited pre-tax assets, the opposite logic applies: prioritize Roth withdrawals for yourself, and designate traditional IRAs for future charitable giving. The "best" sequence is whichever one serves your specific mix of income stability, tax efficiency, and legacy priorities – and stays flexible enough to adapt as laws and life change.

4.2 Coordinating Withdrawals Across Account Types

A preferred order is a good start, but retirement rarely cooperates with neat rules. Markets move unevenly, healthcare events arise, family needs shift, Congress rewrites parts of the tax code periodically. Coordinating withdrawals is an ongoing process, not a one-time decision. Each year is its own small planning exercise: how much do we need? What's this year's income mix? What does that do to our bracket, Social Security taxation, and Medicare premiums — not just now, but down the line?

Monitoring Brackets to Avoid Surprises

Think of each tax bracket as a highway lane. Your goal is staying in the lane that makes sense, using different accounts to avoid drifting into a lane with a much higher marginal rate unless there's a good reason to. A large single-year withdrawal — buying a second home, paying off a mortgage — can catapult you into a higher bracket, and the chain reaction matters as much as the rate itself: higher AGI can raise the taxable share of Social Security, trigger IRMAA two years later, and affect deduction eligibility. Pulling part of that amount from Roth instead, or spreading the expense across two calendar years, can keep taxable income inside the bracket you actually want.

Coordinated withdrawals often mean blending sources deliberately — funding a baseline budget from Social Security, modest traditional distributions, and taxable account income, then covering larger discretionary spending from Roth withdrawals that don't touch AGI at all. Using bracket thresholds as guardrails keeps the plan grounded in the actual tax system rather than guesswork.

Balancing Income to Manage Social Security Taxation

The taxable share of your Social Security benefit — 0%, 50%, or up to 85% — depends on provisional income, which includes half your benefit plus other taxable income and certain tax-exempt interest. Pull too much from pre-tax accounts, and you raise both your ordinary income and the taxable share of your benefit at once. Coordinated withdrawals manage this directly: leaning on Roth and taxable accounts to stay under a threshold, or — in years before Social Security starts — front-loading traditional withdrawals or conversions while there's no Social Security income in the formula at all.

Delaying Social Security to claim a larger check can also reduce pressure on the rest of your portfolio later, giving more room to use Roth or taxable accounts strategically. Claim early instead, and you'll likely be more sensitive to how additional traditional withdrawals affect provisional income. The coordination story isn't about any single year — it's weaving your claiming age and account mix into one coherent, tax-aware pattern.

Managing RMDs Alongside Other Income

RMDs are one of the most rigid elements of retirement tax planning — once you hit the applicable age, you must withdraw at least the IRS-specified amount or face steep penalties, and because RMDs count as taxable income, they can land hard on top of substantial other income.

Planning ahead softens the blow: reduce future RMDs through strategic withdrawals or conversions in the years leading up to RMD age, especially while your rate is temporarily low. Some advisors suggest treating the RMD itself as your retirement "paycheck," then adjusting any additional withdrawals from taxable or Roth only if spending needs exceed it.

Because Medicare premiums use income from two years prior, a large RMD year can mean a higher premium two years later. Coordinating around this — pairing a higher-RMD year with lower discretionary spending elsewhere, or offsetting with more Roth usage — helps avoid needless surcharges. QCDs remain a useful tool here too: directing part of an RMD to charity satisfies the distribution requirement without raising AGI at all.

Recalibrating as Life Changes

Retirement isn't a static glide path. Early retirement often means more travel and active spending; mid-retirement settles into a routine; late retirement often brings rising healthcare costs. Inflation, market performance, and tax law layer on top of all of it — a withdrawal strategy that fit at 65 may be suboptimal by 75, even with a similar total portfolio value.

This is why coordinated withdrawals require ongoing recalibration. Leaning heavily on Roth in your sixties to keep taxes near zero may feel comfortable but can leave a large pre-tax balance and a compressed RMD problem later. Draining taxable accounts too aggressively, ignoring chances to realize gains at favorable rates, can leave money on the table too. Revisit your cash flow needs, bracket position, RMD schedule, and goals every year or two, and adjust the mix from each bucket accordingly. If markets have been strong, you might harvest gains in a low-income year, raising your cost basis. In a weak market, harvest losses instead and lean on safer holdings or tax-deferred accounts. The best plan is a living framework, not a fixed one.

4.3 Managing Capital Gains and Harvesting Losses

Inside taxable accounts specifically, another set of tools can sharpen your tax efficiency further: managing which lots you sell, and when, to actively shape your tax outcome rather than just reacting to it.

Realized Gains and Their Tax Treatment

You don't owe capital gains tax on price appreciation until you sell — at that point, the difference between sale price and cost basis is your realized gain (or loss). Held over a year, it typically qualifies as long-term and gets favorable rates; held a year or less, it's short-term and taxed at your ordinary rate, often a meaningfully higher cost.

This has real implications for withdrawal planning. Prioritize selling long-term positions over short-term ones where possible, and deliberately realize gains during years when other income is low enough to land in the 0% long-term capital gains bracket. In a window before Social Security starts, or after a period of lower earnings, you can harvest gains at low or zero tax cost, reset your basis higher, and reposition toward a more suitable allocation. Conversely, avoid realizing large gains in years when ordinary income is already high from RMDs or other sources — the stacked total could push you into a higher capital gains bracket and aggravate other thresholds at the same time. Understanding how realized gains stack on top of ordinary income lets you pick your moments deliberately rather than by accident.

Tax-Loss Harvesting

Realizing losses can generate tax assets just as realizing gains creates liabilities. Sell an investment below your basis, and you can use that loss to offset gains elsewhere. If losses exceed gains in a given year, you can also use a portion against ordinary income, with any remainder carried forward indefinitely.

This is most valuable in retirement when coordinated with your actual withdrawal needs. If you must sell appreciated assets to fund spending, look across your portfolio for positions currently below cost basis and harvest those losses at the same time — while maintaining your overall market exposure through similar (not identical) replacement holdings. The net effect: you meet your income needs while softening or eliminating the tax bite from the necessary sale. Banked losses also add flexibility later — harvest during a market downturn, and those losses can offset gains you choose to realize once markets recover, or soak up part of the cost of a Roth conversion done in a higher-income year.

Avoiding the Wash Sale Rule

The major caveat: sell a security at a loss, then buy the same or a "substantially identical" security within 30 days before or after, and the loss is disallowed — added back into your basis on the replacement instead of being usable now. Avoid the temptation to sell for the loss and immediately buy back the same thing. Many investors swap into a similar-but-not-identical substitute instead — a different broad index fund tracking a similar but distinct index, for instance — keeping market exposure roughly intact while staying on the right side of the rule. Watch automatic dividend reinvestment and rebalancing trades too; they can accidentally repurchase the same security inside the wash-sale window without you noticing.

Integrating Capital Gains Management Into Your Plan

Done well, gains and losses become active levers rather than fixed outcomes. Align gain realization with bracket management — fill the 0% capital gains bracket in a low-ordinary-income year, then reinvest the proceeds. Deploy loss harvesting during weak markets or ahead of anticipated high-income years, banking a cushion against taxes from necessary portfolio changes or planned conversions.

The bigger point: withdrawal sequencing isn't just about which account you tap first. It's about how every withdrawal — taxable, traditional, or Roth — affects your overall tax picture together. Selling in a taxable account can be tax-efficient or tax-expensive depending on holding period, basis, and offsetting losses. A traditional withdrawal may or may not be costly depending on your current bracket versus your expected future one. Roth money may be ideal one year and unnecessary the next. Seeing all of these as connected, rather than separate decisions, is the actual skill this chapter is teaching.

Smart withdrawal sequencing isn't about memorizing one "right" order. It's understanding how taxable, tax-deferred, and Roth accounts interact with the tax system, Social Security rules, and Medicare thresholds — then using that understanding to build a flexible, adaptive plan. For most households, the default framework — spend from taxable while managing gains, bring in controlled tax-deferred withdrawals or conversions, preserve Roth for later — is a strong starting point. Layer bracket-conscious planning, coordinated Social Security timing, proactive RMD management, and opportunistic gain and loss harvesting around that framework, and you're not just minimizing tax in any single year. You're reducing lifetime tax drag in a way that supports a retirement that actually feels stable. With a thoughtful sequence, your money doesn't just last longer — it works smarter for you at every stage.

Key Takeaways

• The classic order — taxable, then tax-deferred, then Roth — is a strong baseline, but rigid adherence can let tax-deferred accounts grow too large and create an oversized RMD problem later

• Most retirees do best with a hybrid approach: blending withdrawals across all three buckets based on the current year's bracket position, not a fixed sequence

• Roth withdrawals don't count as taxable income and don't affect Social Security taxation or Medicare premiums — making Roth money the most flexible source for large one-time expenses

• Capital losses can offset capital gains, and a limited amount of ordinary income, through tax-loss harvesting

• The wash sale rule disallows a loss if you buy the same or a "substantially identical" security within 30 days before or after the sale

Revisit your withdrawal mix every year or two — a strategy that fit at 65 may not fit at 75, even with a similar portfolio value

Chapter 5: Roth Conversions and When They Make Sense

Chapter at a Glance

What you'll learn in this chapter:

• The real difference between partial and full Roth conversions — and which situations call for each

• How age, health, and legacy goals should change your conversion math

• A practical method for estimating exactly what a conversion will cost you, this year and in ripple effects later

• Two contrasting case studies showing the difference between a planned conversion and a rushed one

Estimated reading time: 28 minutes

> ***FIELD NOTE*** *I've seen retirees do a full six-figure Roth conversion in a single year because they wanted to "just get it over with" — and watched the IRMAA letter arrive eighteen months later with real frustration attached. The conversion wasn't a bad idea. The timing was. This chapter is about getting both right.*

For many people, "Roth conversion" sounds like something only high-net-worth investors or tax geeks need to worry about. In reality, it's simply a choice about when you want to pay tax on money you've already saved. Pay it now, convert to Roth, and enjoy tax-free growth and withdrawals later — or defer the bill and let future-you deal with it. This chapter is about recognizing when that trade is smart, and when it isn't.

Done thoughtfully, conversions can reduce your lifetime tax bill, shrink or eliminate future RMDs, and leave heirs a cleaner, more flexible legacy. Done carelessly, they can spike your tax bracket for a year, raise your Medicare premiums, and create a cash crunch when the bill comes due. A conversion is also generally permanent — once converted, the money can't go back into a traditional IRA — which makes understanding the tradeoffs before you act especially important.

5.1 Partial vs. Full Roth Conversions

A conversion moves money from a traditional IRA or 401(k) into a Roth account, and the amount moved is added to your taxable income for that year. There's no early withdrawal penalty just for converting, but there is a tax bill. After that, the money sits in the Roth, growing and eventually coming out tax-free if you follow the rules. The strategic question is whether to convert everything at once, or in smaller slices over time.

Partial Conversions

Partial conversions move only a portion of your balance in any given year — the approach most retirees and near-retirees use, because it offers fine-tuned control over how much extra income shows up on a given year's return.

The central advantage is spreading the tax impact. Say you have a $600,000 traditional IRA. Converting it all at once could catapult you into the highest federal brackets and trigger extra state tax, Medicare surcharges, and the phase-out of certain deductions. Converting $50,000 to $100,000 a year instead lets you fill lower brackets without spilling into much higher ones — keeping the marginal rate on each conversion dollar under your control.

Partial conversions are especially useful for staying under a target bracket ceiling or an IRMAA threshold. Every bracket has a ceiling — the top dollar it can absorb before spilling into the next. A partial conversion lets you convert right up to that ceiling without crossing it. They also leave room for ongoing reassessment: tax laws change, markets move, your situation shifts. Converting gradually means you can review annually — did income come in higher or lower than expected? Did Congress adjust the brackets? Is this a good year because markets are temporarily down? You're not locked into a ten-year plan made on day one.

One more advantage: each conversion starts its own five-year clock for penalty-free access if you're under 59½. If you think you might need some converted principal early, or want to track multiple "vintages" of conversions, smaller chunks over time make the rules easier to navigate without accidentally triggering a 10% penalty.

When Full Conversions Make Sense

Converting an entire account in one year is a bolder move — it concentrates the tax hit into a single calendar year, which can be painful, but sometimes the pain is worth it.

One obvious scenario: a year when your taxable income is unusually low — a layoff, a sold business, or the gap years right after retirement before Social Security and pensions begin. With less other income on the return, there's room in the lower brackets to absorb a large conversion without hitting top rates.

A second scenario: you're about to move to a higher-tax state but still have a year or two left in a low-tax or no-tax one. Converting while you're still a resident of the no-tax state can avoid state tax on the conversion entirely, even though future withdrawals would otherwise have been taxed in your new home. The same logic applies if you expect federal rates to rise significantly — from scheduled law changes, or because your own income will climb later due to pensions, business income, or large RMDs.

A full conversion also simplifies your future: once the account is entirely Roth, RMDs on that money disappear, and you no longer juggle multiple account types and tax treatments in later retirement. For people who value simplicity, or who have strong legacy goals, that clean sweep can feel worth the upfront cost.

The downside is real, though. All converted dollars are taxed as ordinary income in one year — potentially pushing you into much higher brackets, exposing more Social Security to tax, raising state tax, and triggering IRMAA surcharges for a year or two. If you're not careful, the combined effect can erode much of the conversion's benefit, which is why even committed Roth advocates often stage conversions over several years instead of doing it all at once.

Age and Time Horizon

Younger retirees — late fifties or early sixties — usually have a long runway before RMDs begin and a long horizon for Roth assets to compound. For them, partial conversions spread over many years tend to work best: chip away during low-income years, let the converted dollars grow tax-free for decades.

Closer to RMD age, the calculus shifts. At 70, staring at large RMDs in a few years, more aggressive conversion moves sooner — even accepting higher upfront tax — can meaningfully shrink the RMD problem waiting at 73 or 75. Life expectancy matters too: conversions generally pay off more the longer the money sits undisturbed. A 60-year-old in good health, expecting to live into their late eighties and hoping to leave money to children, has decades to recoup the upfront cost. An 80-year-old in fragile health may not get enough benefit from the extra growth to justify a large conversion.

Legacy intentions shape the decision further. If your heirs are likely to be in high brackets themselves, converting more aggressively can be an act of tax-efficient generosity — you pay the conversion tax at your rate, sparing them higher ordinary income tax on inherited traditional withdrawals. If much of your estate is headed to charity instead, the opposite logic applies: leave pre-tax accounts to the charity, which owes no income tax on distributions, and keep Roth or taxable assets for individual heirs.

Balancing Financial Goals and Tax Liability

The first practical question is whether you can pay the conversion tax without tapping the account itself. Using IRA or 401(k) funds to cover the tax bill shrinks the amount left to grow tax-free, and if you're under 59½, it can trigger an extra 10% penalty on those withdrawn funds.

Consider how a conversion interacts with your other income in a given year. Significant wages, business income, or capital gains might mean limiting conversions to avoid an uncomfortably high total. Conversely, if you know a future year includes a one-time spike — a property sale, exercised stock options — front-loading conversions into earlier, lower-income years makes sense.

Liquidity matters too. Ideally, pay the conversion tax with cash you're comfortable spending — not by selling investments you'd rather keep, or creating capital gains you were trying to avoid in the first place. And check your estate documents and beneficiary designations before converting aggressively: if your plan already earmarks pre-tax accounts for charity and other assets for individuals, an aggressive conversion strategy might introduce tax nobody needed to pay.

5.2 Timing Conversions to Control Bracket Creep

Because conversions are taxed as ordinary income, their effect on your bracket is immediate and visible. "Bracket creep" is the way extra income — like a large conversion — can quietly push more of your other income into higher brackets, even when your actual lifestyle hasn't changed. Thoughtful timing is what keeps a smart long-term move from becoming a short-term shock.

Managing Bracket Thresholds

Every bracket has a floor and ceiling, and your marginal rate applies only to the last dollar — not the whole amount. Conversion income stacks on top of wages, pensions, Social Security, and everything else, so the more you stack, the more dollars risk landing in the next bracket up.

The practical method: estimate your taxable income for the year without any conversion — wages, pensions, interest, dividends, gains, minus deductions — and see where that lands relative to your bracket ceiling. Suppose you're in the 22% bracket, which tops out at $100,000, and your projected income without a conversion is $80,000. You have about $20,000 of headroom. Convert roughly that amount, and the whole conversion stays at 22%. Convert more, and the excess gets taxed at the next bracket's rate. Some retirees are comfortable crossing into the next bracket intentionally; others prefer capping conversions right at the ceiling every year. Either is reasonable — what matters is choosing on purpose rather than by accident. Many advisors suggest waiting until later in the year, once you have real visibility into total income, before finalizing the exact amount.

Spreading Conversions Over Multiple Years

This is usually the most powerful way to avoid bracket creep. Instead of one large conversion blasting you into much higher brackets, a series of modest conversions fills your chosen bracket every year — the total converted may end up the same, but the average rate paid can be meaningfully lower.

This also keeps AGI more stable, which limits how much of Social Security becomes taxable and reduces Medicare surcharge risk, while staying adaptable: speed up if laws shift favorably, slow down if a new income source appears, convert more if markets dip and asset values are temporarily low. If you retire at 62 with no pension or Social Security yet, you might convert enough each year from 62 to 70 to use your lower brackets fully — before Social Security and RMDs arrive and raise your bracket for good. By front-loading conversions into the years your rate is lowest, you've captured the window while it was open.

This doesn't require rigid commitment. Plan to convert a set amount annually for a decade, but if year three brings an unplanned rental sale with a large gain, skip or reduce that year's conversion. The point is retaining control, adjusting as new information arrives.

Taking Advantage of Low-Income Years

Some years are simply better for conversions — by design or by circumstance. Early retirement is the classic example: retire at 60, delay Social Security to 70, and you may have a decade where your primary income is a taxable brokerage account or cash savings, your bracket far lower than during your working years or once RMDs begin. Converting during this window locks in low rates on dollars that would otherwise be taxed later at higher ones — voluntarily filling your low brackets now instead of leaving the space unused and facing forced distributions at higher rates down the road. This can be especially efficient for couples with staggered retirements, where one spouse's earlier exit creates a temporary dip in joint income.

Unexpected low-income years — a sabbatical, a career break, a business downturn, or a year with offsetting investment losses — create the same opportunity. Market downturns themselves are conversion opportunities, since you're taxed on asset value at the time of conversion: convert a depressed holding you still believe in, and the eventual rebound happens inside the tax-free Roth instead of a taxable account.

Case Studies and Example Timelines

Maria retires at 63 with $800,000 in traditional IRAs and modest taxable savings, planning to delay Social Security until 70. From 63 to 69, she lives mostly off taxable accounts, with projected taxable income around $30,000 a year — comfortably within a lower bracket that tops out near $60,000. She converts $25,000 to $30,000 annually. Over seven years, she moves roughly $200,000 into a Roth at modest marginal rates. At 73, when RMDs start, her traditional IRA balance is substantially smaller — and so are the taxes on her forced withdrawals.

Henry decides at 68 that he wants to "just get it over with" and converts his entire $500,000 IRA in a single year, on top of $80,000 of pension income. The conversion drives his taxable income into much higher federal brackets and triggers IRMAA surcharges two years later, raising his Medicare premiums for a full year. The long-term benefit of having Roth assets is still real, but his average tax rate on the conversion dollars is far higher than it would have been with a phased approach. Had he converted a smaller amount annually starting at 65, he could have reached a similar Roth balance while keeping his brackets moderate the whole way through.

Notice the less obvious ripple effects in Henry's case: higher income from the conversion pushed more Social Security into the taxable column and could, in other circumstances, affect financial aid calculations for a grandchild or eligibility for certain tax credits. Maria's steady, moderate approach avoided every one of those cliffs while making just as much long-term progress reshaping her tax picture.

5.3 Estimating Costs and Reducing Future RMDs

Calculating the Tax Liability

The mechanics are straightforward: the converted amount is added to your taxable income for the year and taxed at your marginal ordinary rate. There's no 10% early distribution penalty just for converting, regardless of age — but any separate withdrawal you take from the IRA to pay that tax may itself be treated as a taxable distribution, and if you're under 59½, that portion could face a penalty.

A simple estimation method: calculate your taxable income without the conversion, identify your current bracket and how far you are from its ceiling, then add the proposed conversion amount and see where the new total lands. The portion that fits inside your existing bracket gets taxed at that rate; anything spilling into the next bracket gets taxed at the higher rate. Sum the pieces for your total estimated conversion tax.

Example: in the 22% bracket, converting $20,000 that fits entirely within that bracket costs roughly $4,400 in federal tax. If part of it spills into the 24% bracket instead, you'd pay 22% on the portion that fits and 24% on the spillover. State tax, where applicable, adds another layer — high-tax states can meaningfully raise the real cost of a conversion, which is one reason some people convert more aggressively while living in a low-tax state, or before a planned move.

Beyond the direct tax, higher reported income in the conversion year can ripple outward: raising your state tax bill, phasing out certain deductions or credits, increasing the taxable share of Social Security, and triggering higher Medicare premiums two years later via IRMAA. Factor in these indirect effects, not just the sticker price on the converted amount.

How Conversions Reduce Future RMDs

Every dollar converted from a traditional account to Roth is a dollar that will never generate an RMD. Roth IRAs carry no RMDs for the original owner under current rules, which means strategic conversions in your sixties and early seventies can meaningfully shrink the size of your future mandatory withdrawals — and the tax liability that comes with them. For retirees who don't need RMDs to cover living expenses and would rather leave the money invested, this materially improves long-term tax efficiency.

Smaller future RMDs help control other triggers too — lower taxable income in later years can mean a lower bracket, less Social Security taxed, and more room below IRMAA thresholds. In effect, a carefully planned conversion swaps a series of forced future distributions for a flexible pool of Roth assets you can tap, or ignore, entirely on your own terms.

There's a legacy angle as well. Beneficiaries who inherit a traditional IRA generally must deplete it within ten years, paying ordinary income tax on every withdrawal. Inherit a Roth IRA instead, and the same ten-year window applies, but the withdrawals are typically tax-free. Conversions during your lifetime function as a form of tax prepayment on behalf of children or grandchildren who might otherwise pay at a higher rate than you would today.

State and Medicare Implications

Conversions are usually treated as taxable income at the state level too, where applicable. Living in a high-tax state now but planning to move to a low- or no-tax state later? It may make sense to delay larger conversions until after the move. The reverse holds too — enjoying a temporary stint in a no-tax state before returning to a taxed one is a good reason to convert more now.

Medicare premiums deserve their own line item in this math, since IRMAA is based on income from two years prior — large conversions can push you above the threshold for at least a year. These surcharges are rarely catastrophic in dollar terms, but they're real, and timing conversions before Medicare enrollment, or smoothing them to only occasionally cross an IRMAA threshold, helps control the impact.

Conversion-driven income can also raise the taxable share of Social Security through the same provisional income mechanism covered in Chapter 2. For retirees already receiving benefits, it's often more efficient to do the heavier conversions before benefits begin – using the early retirement years as a tax sandbox, free of that added complication.

Because federal tax, state tax, Medicare, and Social Security interlock in ways that aren't always obvious, modeling a few different timelines – even a basic projection of expected RMDs, brackets, and IRMAA status with and without conversions – can clarify which approach actually leaves you with more after-tax income over time.

Long-Term Benefits vs. Upfront Costs

A Roth conversion is, at bottom, a trade: a known, immediate cost for a potential long-term benefit. Think in terms of a breakeven period – how long the money needs to stay in the Roth before tax-free growth and lower RMDs outweigh the upfront tax. Precise numbers depend on assumed returns and future tax rates, but a few rules of thumb help.

If your current marginal rate is clearly lower than what you expect to face later on RMDs or other distributions, conversions tend to make sense – you're buying out of future higher taxes at today's lower price, especially if you can pay the conversion tax from a relatively tax-inefficient taxable account that would have been taxed annually anyway. If you expect your future rate to be significantly lower instead – modest spending needs, large deductions, charitable bequests of pre-tax accounts – the case for aggressive conversion weakens considerably; paying a high rate now to avoid a low rate later rarely adds up. Smaller "micro-conversions" filling only the lowest brackets, or no conversion at all, may be the more sensible path.

The five-year rule factors into the calculus too – converted amounts generally need to stay in the Roth at least five years, or until 59½, to avoid penalties on withdrawn principal. If you're likely to need the money sooner, or you're already well into your seventies with limited time for compounding, the breakeven period may simply be too long to make sense.

In most real-world plans, the answer lands somewhere in the middle: convert enough each year to build meaningful tax diversification alongside your traditional and taxable accounts, without feeling compelled to move everything. That diversification gives your future self more levers — lean on Roth in high-income years, draw from pre-tax accounts (and maybe convert a bit more) in low-income ones. The goal isn't a perfect number. It's giving yourself options.

Key Takeaways

• A Roth conversion is generally permanent — once converted, the money cannot go back into a traditional IRA

• Partial conversions, spread over several years, usually produce a lower average tax rate than one large conversion in a single year

• The "fill the bracket" technique — converting only up to the ceiling of your current bracket — keeps the marginal rate on the conversion under your control

• Age, health, and legacy goals all change the math: younger and healthier retirees generally benefit more from conversions, since the money has longer to compound tax-free

• Converted funds generally need to stay in the Roth for five years, or until age 59½, to avoid a penalty on withdrawn principal

• Every dollar converted is a dollar that will never generate an RMD — conversions done in your sixties can meaningfully shrink the size of future required distributions

Chapter 6: Tax Bracket Management: Using Margins to Your Advantage

Chapter at a Glance

What you'll learn in this chapter:

• Why "filling" a lower bracket on purpose almost always beats waiting to see what happens

• How to harvest capital gains at 0% tax by paying attention to where your other income lands

• Building a multi-year income projection that actually predicts your RMD-era tax spike before it arrives

• The "widow's penalty" — and why converting while both spouses are alive can prevent it

Estimated reading time: 27 minutes

FIELD NOTE *The retirees who handle this well don't think of tax brackets as something to avoid. They think of them as shelf space — and they make sure none of it goes to waste. That single mental shift is most of what this chapter is trying to teach.*

Most people think about tax brackets simply: "I'm in the 22% bracket," or "I don't want to get pushed into the 24% bracket." Understandable, but limiting. In retirement, managing taxes is less about avoiding a specific bracket at all costs and more about using each bracket's space deliberately, year after year. Do that, and the tax code becomes less of a threat and more of a tool you can bend in your favor.

Picture your brackets as a series of shelves. Each holds a certain amount of income before it overflows onto the next shelf, taxed at a higher rate. You never pay your top rate on every dollar — only on whatever spills onto that top shelf. If you can see how full each shelf is, you can decide which dollars to recognize this year, which to delay, and which to convert into more tax-friendly forms.

We've already seen how overreliance on the tax-deferred bucket can backfire later, when RMDs, Social Security taxation, and Medicare surcharges collide all at once. This chapter builds directly on the withdrawal sequencing from Chapter 4: mapping your income across multiple years, deliberately filling lower brackets, and avoiding the sudden jumps in tax rate or Medicare premium that catch people off guard.

6.1 Proactive Bracket Planning and "Filling" Lower Brackets

A useful reframe: stop asking "how do I pay the least tax this year?" and start asking "what's the best way to use my brackets over my entire retirement?" Those are different questions. Focusing only on this year tempts you to defer tax-deferred withdrawals as long as possible, keeping early-retirement income artificially low. That feels satisfying right up until RMDs, Social Security, and pensions push your later-life income so high that you land in an equal or higher bracket than you were ever in while working — paying more total tax, plus higher Medicare premiums and Social Security taxation on top.

The core idea: intentionally fill your lower brackets each year with income you can control — IRA withdrawals, Roth conversions — instead of waiting for the government to force withdrawals at a less convenient time. That sometimes means paying some tax earlier than strictly necessary, but that's often the price of avoiding bracket creep: the gradual drift of more income into higher brackets as balances grow and mandatory distributions begin.

Marginal Rates, Revisited

Your "tax bracket" is the rate on your last dollar of income, not the rate on all of it. If your taxable income sits well below the top of the 12% bracket, that unused capacity on the shelf is a missed opportunity — dollars you could pull from a traditional IRA or convert at 12% now, rather than risking they get taxed at 22% or higher later once RMDs, Social Security, and a possible single-filer transition all stack on top.

The difference between marginal and effective rate matters here too. Your marginal rate is what applies to your next dollar; your effective rate is total tax divided by total income. Strategic bracket management focuses on the marginal rate, because that's where the real decision about an extra $10,000, $20,000, or $50,000 actually lives. Once you know how much room remains before the next bracket, you can use it on purpose — matching controllable income to available bracket space.

Using Partial Withdrawals Instead of One Big One

A large one-time distribution — for a home project, a car, a trip — taken without planning can push chunks of income into higher brackets, raising not just the tax bill but the taxable share of Social Security and the odds of an IRMAA surcharge. A more efficient approach: spread withdrawals across several years, intentionally filling your 10%, 12%, or 22% bracket rather than waiting for RMD age and taking whatever the formula dictates. This shrinks the account before RMDs begin, can reduce future required distributions, and stays flexible if tax law or your spending needs shift.

Consider someone retiring at 65, delaying Social Security until 70, with no pension. In those gap years, taxable income might be quite low — an ideal window to draw from tax-deferred accounts deliberately, up to a chosen bracket limit, investing whatever isn't needed for spending in a taxable or Roth account instead of leaving that low-bracket space unused.

Harvesting Gains Within Lower Brackets

Bracket management isn't only about ordinary income — it applies to capital gains too. Long-term gains and qualified dividends have their own tiered structure: 0% in some income ranges, 15% or 20% in others, plus the 3.8% NIIT surtax for higher earners. In a low-income year, you can harvest appreciated holdings in a taxable account up to the top of a favorable bracket — resetting your cost basis higher while paying little or no tax — and, if you want to keep the same position, immediately buy back the same or a similar investment.

The key is overlaying your capital gains strategy on top of your ordinary income picture: ordinary income fills the brackets first, and whatever room remains determines how much room exists for gains at the lower rate. This is especially useful if you expect higher income in later years from RMDs or a property sale, or if you expect rates to rise. It also supports other goals — funding a donor-advised fund with appreciated securities, for instance, removes future taxable gains while creating a charitable deduction in the year of the gift.

Timing Other Income Events

Not all retirement income is fully under your control, but more of it is flexible than it first appears. Social Security claiming age is a major lever. Pension elections sometimes allow choosing a start age or a lump sum versus an annuity. Annuities, deferred compensation, and even continued part-time work can all be timed.

Coordinating the timing of these streams smooths your taxable income across years instead of bunching too much into one. If you know that age 70 brings both Social Security and a deferred compensation payout, you might draw more from your IRA between 65 and 69 specifically to use those lower-income years before the other sources arrive. Planning a property or business sale similarly benefits from choosing a year with minimal competing income, or structuring the sale as an installment arrangement across multiple years.

6.2 Multi-Year Income Smoothing and Tax-Loss Harvesting

So far we've looked mostly at single-year decisions. The real power of bracket management comes from stitching those decisions into a coherent multi-year strategy — retirement can last 20, 30, even 40 years, tax laws will change, markets will move, and a one-year mindset simply isn't enough.

Multi-year income smoothing means designing your income pattern to avoid extreme highs and lows. Instead of near-zero taxable income in your sixties followed by large compulsory RMDs in your seventies and eighties, you aim for a more level path — filling lower brackets earlier, reducing future RMDs, keeping future brackets and surcharges in check.

Building a Long-Term Income Projection

Start with the building blocks: Social Security (including planned claiming ages for you and a spouse), pensions, annuities, estimated RMDs, rental income, and any continued earnings. Layer on the controllable pieces: planned IRA withdrawals, Roth conversions, taxable account withdrawals, and any large one-time events like selling a home or business. Even a simplified version of this projection reveals when your income is likely to surge or dip — you'll often see that taxable income stays low from 65 to 70, then rises sharply once Social Security and RMDs both kick in. That observation is what drives the action: using the low years deliberately, before the spike arrives, to smooth the whole curve.

Strategic Conversions Over Multiple Years

Roth conversions are one of the most powerful multi-year smoothing tools available, for all the reasons covered in Chapter 5 — but the framing here is slightly different. Rather than asking "should I convert," the multi-year question is "how much unused bracket space do I have this year, and does converting into it make sense given everything else going on?" Calculate the room before the next bracket, convert roughly that amount, reassess next year, and repeat. As you convert, you're moving assets from the tax-deferred bucket to the tax-free one — often using taxable-bucket cash to pay the resulting tax, preserving more of the Roth for long-term growth.

There's a specific scenario worth flagging here: the "widow's penalty." After one spouse dies, the survivor typically moves from married-filing-jointly to single status, which can push the same dollar amount of income into a higher bracket than it would have faced before. Converting more aggressively while both spouses are alive and joint brackets are still wider can meaningfully reduce the taxable balance the survivor will eventually have to draw down alone.

Using Losses to Create Room

While conversions and bracket-filling withdrawals are about adding income deliberately, loss harvesting is about creating space. In years when markets decline, selling depressed holdings in taxable accounts generates losses that offset gains — and, within limits, ordinary income — elsewhere. If you want to realize long-term gains to reset your basis but worry about a higher capital gains rate, harvested losses already on hand can neutralize part or all of that gain, keeping you inside your target rate. The same wash sale caution from Chapter 4 applies here: sell a losing position and replace it with something similar but not identical, preserving your allocation while keeping the loss usable.

Adjusting for Market and Life Events

No plan survives contact with real life perfectly intact. In a lower-income year than expected — a delayed property sale, less work than planned, a market downturn that reduces interest and dividends — you might convert more or realize more gains than originally planned. In a higher-income year — capital gains distributions, a business sale, a one-time payout — you might back off conversions and lean on loss harvesting or Roth funds instead. This is a rebalancing exercise, not a set-and-forget plan: check where you stand relative to your projected path each year, and adjust.

6.3 Estimating and Managing Taxable Income Windows

A "window" is the range of taxable income that keeps you within a target bracket, accounting for both ordinary income and capital gains, plus the thresholds that matter for other surcharges. Instead of "I'm in the 22% bracket," the more useful question becomes: how far into it am I, how much room remains before 24%, and where are the breakpoints for Social Security taxation, IRMAA, and capital gains rate changes?

Identify the brackets relevant to your filing status — typically 10%, 12%, 22%, 24%, and possibly higher — along with the capital gains rate breakpoints and the NIIT threshold if you're in higher income territory. Beyond the basic brackets, a handful of thresholds create genuine "cliffs": cross one, and a single extra dollar of income can trigger hundreds or thousands in extra tax or premium, all at once. Because the IRS adjusts brackets and many thresholds annually for inflation, refresh this list every year — you don't need to memorize every line, just know roughly where your target brackets begin and end.

Monitoring as the Year Progresses

Many retirees wait until tax time to find out where they landed — too late to change anything. A better habit is checking in periodically, perhaps quarterly, on projected taxable income: a simple spreadsheet update with year-to-date withdrawals, pension income, expected Social Security, portfolio income, and realized gains and losses covers most of it. If you're approaching the top of your target bracket sooner than expected, slow down withdrawals or postpone a planned conversion. If you're well under it late in the year, accelerate — complete an additional conversion, realize more gains — to use the available window before it closes for the year. This kind of mid-year check-in also catches opportunities that would otherwise slip by, like a sudden market dip that opens up loss harvesting, or an unexpected bonus that temporarily raises income.

Coordinating Timing Across Income Types

All of these threads — thresholds, monitoring, multi-year projections — come together when you coordinate timing across income types directly. Ordinary income from pensions, wages, and IRA withdrawals stacks differently than long-term gains, qualified dividends, and tax-free Roth withdrawals; some income (Roth distributions) may not count as taxable at all, while others (RMDs, annuity payouts) are largely or entirely taxable. Knowing which counts where gives you the power to keep total taxable income inside your chosen window. In a year with higher expected ordinary income — RMDs, a pension lump sum — cover extra spending from Roth instead of additional IRA withdrawals, preventing taxable income from creeping into the next bracket. In a lower-income year, do the reverse: draw from traditional accounts and convert, while letting Roth rest untouched.

The order in which you tap taxable, tax-deferred, and tax-free accounts, introduced in Chapter 4, gets more nuanced here. It's not "always spend taxable first" as a rigid rule — it's a flexible framework where you vary the mix based on where you currently sit relative to your taxable income windows. Sometimes you lean on taxable accounts for favorable capital gains rates; sometimes on tax-deferred accounts to fill lower ordinary brackets; sometimes on Roth funds specifically to avoid a bracket jump or surcharge at a critical moment.

In practice, effective tax bracket management is an ongoing conversation between your goals, your spending needs, the current rules, and the shape of your income over time. It links directly back to tax diversification and withdrawal order from earlier chapters, and it sets up the legacy and charitable planning ahead. Understand your brackets, use the margins on purpose, and revisit the plan every year — and taxes stop being an unpredictable drag and become a manageable, even strategic, part of how your retirement actually plays out.

Key Takeaways

• Think of tax brackets as shelves — only the dollars on a given shelf are taxed at that shelf's rate, and unused shelf space in a low bracket is a missed opportunity if left empty

• "Filling" a lower bracket deliberately with IRA withdrawals or Roth conversions usually beats waiting and letting RMDs fill it for you later, often at a higher rate

• Long-term capital gains and qualified dividends have their own tiered rates — sometimes 0% — and can be harvested in low-income years for little or no tax cost

• A "taxable income window" is the range that keeps you inside a target bracket once both ordinary income and capital gains are accounted for

• The "widow's penalty" — moving from married-filing-jointly to single after a spouse's death — can push the same income into a higher bracket; converting more while both spouses are alive helps reduce this later impact

• Multi-year income projections reveal income spikes (RMDs plus Social Security arriving together, for example) years before they actually happen, giving you time to smooth them out

Quick Check-In

By now, you've covered some of the most important foundations of retirement tax strategy planning.

If this guide is helping you feel more clear or confident about your next steps—even in a small way—consider leaving a short review once you reach the end.

Even a brief 1–2 sentence review can make a meaningful difference and help others discover this resource.

Let's keep going.

Chapter 7: Medicare, IRMAA, and Other Means-Tested Costs

Chapter at a Glance

What you'll learn in this chapter:

• How Medicare Part B and Part D premiums actually work before any surcharge gets added

• IRMAA's two-year lookback and "cliff" structure — and why one dollar can cost you hundreds

• What counts toward your MAGI for IRMAA purposes, and which income sources quietly don't

• How to coordinate Roth conversions, RMDs, and spousal income to stay under the thresholds you control

Estimated reading time: 29 minutes

> ***FIELD NOTE*** *The Medicare surcharge letter never arrives in the year you made the decision that caused it. It arrives two years later, addressed to a version of you who's already moved on financially. That delay is exactly why so few people connect the dots — and exactly why this chapter exists.*

For many retirees, the surprise doesn't come from a big tax bill. It comes from a letter in the mail. The envelope looks routine, but inside is a notice explaining that your Medicare premiums are going up — sometimes by hundreds of dollars a month — because your income crossed a line you didn't know existed. That line is the Income-Related Monthly Adjustment Amount, or IRMAA, and it's one of the most important, least understood moving parts in retirement income planning.

This chapter makes that line visible. You'll see how Medicare premiums actually work, how income is measured for IRMAA, and why even a one-dollar increase in reported income can trigger a much larger increase in healthcare costs. Then we turn to strategy: shaping and timing income, using Roth accounts and other tools, and coordinating Social Security and RMDs so you're not unintentionally volunteering for higher premiums.

You don't need to become a Medicare expert to benefit here. You just need a working sense of what counts as income, when it's measured, and how it flows through to the premiums deducted from your Social Security check or billed directly to you. Once you see the mechanics, IRMAA stops looking like a random penalty and starts looking like one more dial you can influence with planning.

7.1 How Medicare Premiums and IRMAA Surcharges Are Determined

Understanding Base Medicare Premiums

Medicare has several parts, but IRMAA only touches Parts B and D. Part B covers outpatient and physician services — doctor visits, lab tests, durable medical equipment, many preventive services. Part D covers prescription drugs, either through a standalone plan or as part of Medicare Advantage. Both charge ongoing monthly premiums, and those premiums are the foundation IRMAA builds on.

Each year, Medicare sets a standard Part B premium, and higher-income beneficiaries pay additional surcharges on top. For 2026, the standard Part B premium is $202.90 a month. IRMAA is calculated from your modified adjusted gross income (MAGI) two years prior — for 2026 premiums, Social Security generally looks at your 2024 tax return. For single filers, IRMAA begins above $109,000 of MAGI; for married couples filing jointly, above $218,000. Above those thresholds, both Part B and Part D costs rise in stepped tiers, and because the structure works on a cliff basis within each tier, even a modest amount of extra income can raise your Medicare costs for the full year.

Part D works a bit differently — the base premium is plan-specific, since each drug plan sets its own price. The IRMAA surcharge for Part D sits on top of whatever plan you choose: if you're not subject to IRMAA, you pay your plan's premium only; if you are, you pay that premium plus an income-related surcharge that goes directly to Medicare.

Every IRMAA calculation starts from these base premiums — it adds to them, never replaces them. When someone says they "pay $500 a month for Part B," that usually means the standard premium plus a substantial IRMAA surcharge, all because their income landed in a higher bracket.

The Trigger for IRMAA Surcharges

IRMAA exists because Medicare is partly means-tested: higher-income beneficiaries are asked to shoulder a larger share of the program's cost. The mechanism is a series of income brackets defined by law and adjusted periodically. For each bracket above the base level, the beneficiary's share of cost rises and the government's subsidy falls — at the highest tier, individuals with MAGI at or above $500,000 and couples at or above $750,000 can be required to cover up to 85% of the estimated total cost of Part B coverage. Relatively few retirees reach those levels, but the structure underscores the broader design: the highest earners shoulder the largest share.

IRMAA applies on a strict cliff basis. One dollar below a threshold, you owe no surcharge for that tier. One dollar above, you owe the full surcharge for the entire year — there's no gradual phase-in. That cliff structure is what makes careful income management so powerful, and why a seemingly small decision, like realizing an extra capital gain late in the year, can have a disproportionately large effect on your Medicare costs two years later.

What Counts as Income for IRMAA

To manage IRMAA, you need to understand exactly what's being measured. It starts with your AGI and adds back certain types of income that are normally tax-exempt, like municipal bond interest and some foreign-source income.

Your AGI itself is broad: traditional IRA and 401(k) distributions, pension payments, annuity income, wages, taxable interest, dividends, capital gains, rental income, and the taxable portion of Social Security all flow into it. If you do a Roth conversion, the converted amount is included in AGI for that year — even though future Roth withdrawals will be tax-free, the conversion itself is fully visible to the IRMAA calculation.

On top of AGI, tax-exempt interest gets added back. Many retirees favor municipal bonds because the interest avoids regular federal income tax – but for IRMAA purposes, that interest still counts, because it's added back to arrive at MAGI. You can build a meticulously tax-efficient portfolio and still discover it's pushing you over a Medicare threshold.

Some income genuinely doesn't count, and those exceptions become planning tools. Qualified Roth withdrawals don't increase AGI and therefore don't increase MAGI. HSA withdrawals used for qualified medical expenses are tax-free and don't appear in MAGI either. Return of principal from a non-retirement brokerage account – spending down your original investment rather than realized gains – isn't income at all. These distinctions let you shape your cash flow so you have the money you need without inflating the figure Medicare actually cares about.

Other Means-Tested Costs Beyond IRMAA

IRMAA is the best-known example of Medicare means-testing, but not the only one. For lower-income beneficiaries, Medicare Savings Programs can help cover some or all of the Part B premium and, in some cases, deductibles and coinsurance – administered by state Medicaid agencies, each with its own income and resource limits. Extra Help, the Part D Low-Income Subsidy, reduces prescription drug premiums and copayments for those with limited income and assets. There are also Medicaid programs for people who are "dual eligible," qualifying for both based on age or disability and income.

Because these programs are means-tested too, even modest income increases can affect eligibility – which means careful planning matters not only for higher-income retirees managing IRMAA, but also for those near the margins of these benefit programs on the other end of the income spectrum. You're navigating a landscape of thresholds, some tax-related and some benefit-related, and they need to be seen together rather than in isolation.

7.2 Proactive Strategies to Reduce or Avoid Means-Tested Surcharges

Knowing how IRMAA works is only the first step. The real opportunity comes from using that knowledge to design your income pattern over time. The two-year lookback and cliff-based brackets give you real leverage if you're willing to think ahead and sometimes accept a strategic tax cost in one year to reduce costs across several future years.

Income Timing to Manage IRMAA Triggers

Because IRMAA is determined from income two years prior, timing is everything — when you realize income can matter as much as how much. Plan a large traditional IRA distribution to renovate your home, and if that year becomes the reference year for future premiums, you could push your MAGI over a threshold and raise your Part B and D costs for an entire year.

One workaround is shifting distributions outside the key lookback years. For someone approaching 65, the years at 63 and 64 are especially critical, since they feed directly into Medicare premiums at 65 and 66. Accelerating income into earlier years — age 61 or 62, when it will never touch Medicare — can reduce the need for large taxable withdrawals once you're inside the IRMAA zone. If you anticipate an income spike from a business sale or severance, delaying Medicare enrollment (if you have other coverage) or structuring the event across multiple tax years can have the same protective effect.

Forecasting is the real engine here. Build a multi-year income map: estimated RMDs, expected Social Security, likely capital gains, planned one-time events. Plot how those interact with projected IRMAA thresholds, and you'll start to see which years are relatively safe to realize more income and which ones aren't.

Sometimes you'll accept an IRMAA trigger as the lesser of two evils — it may still be worth realizing a large gain or taking a sizable distribution if the alternative is leaving yourself with painfully high required distributions later that keep you in higher brackets for years.

The goal is deciding consciously, with the trade-off in full view, rather than stumbling into a hidden line by accident.

Using Roth Conversions Strategically

Roth conversions are one of the most powerful long-term IRMAA management tools. You pay tax on the converted amount in the conversion year; after that, qualified withdrawals are tax-free, don't count toward MAGI, and carry no RMDs during the original owner's lifetime.

A well-timed conversion is a way of pre-paying tax in years when your income is relatively low, or before you've entered the Medicare system at all. You accept higher MAGI — and potentially IRMAA — in the conversion year in exchange for lower taxable income and lower IRMAA risk in every future year. Once you're drawing down savings in retirement, Roth withdrawals don't disturb the income line Medicare is watching.

The challenge is avoiding excessive spikes. A single large conversion can easily push you into a high IRMAA tier on top of a higher marginal tax rate — an unpleasant combination. Spreading conversions over several years, each time filling a tax bracket without crossing the next IRMAA threshold, is usually the more effective approach.

There's also a genuine sweet spot in the early retirement window — after you stop working but before claiming Social Security or enrolling in Medicare. Income tends to run low here, especially if you're living partly on after-tax savings, and if you're more than two years from Medicare enrollment, you can convert without worrying about IRMAA at all. Conversions done in this window can meaningfully shrink the size of your future required distributions, and with them, your long-term Medicare premiums.

Coordinating Social Security with Other Income

The way you coordinate Social Security with other income sources also shapes IRMAA exposure, since the taxable portion of your benefit flows into AGI and then into MAGI. Delaying Social Security can reduce MAGI in the early years of retirement — both because you're not yet receiving the benefit and because you may be relying more on income sources that aren't fully taxable.

Delaying to age 70, while drawing from taxable brokerage accounts and Roth IRAs to cover your late-60s spending, keeps reported income lower during the years right around Medicare enrollment — potentially low enough to stay below IRMAA thresholds. Later, once you do claim and your benefit is higher thanks to delayed retirement credits, you may need to draw less heavily on tax-deferred accounts, which again helps manage MAGI.

This is about seeing cash flows holistically. Before a large traditional IRA withdrawal, ask how it interacts with Social Security, pensions, and investment income already in the picture. Could a blend of smaller taxable withdrawals and Roth distributions meet the same need? Would this year — when other income is lower — be a better time to realize a long-term gain than next year, once Social Security or RMDs have started? Asking these questions in advance avoids the cascade effect where one income decision unexpectedly pulls multiple levers at once.

Appealing IRMAA Determinations

Sometimes income drops sharply after a reference year — retirement, the loss of a spouse, divorce, some other life-changing event — and Medicare premiums still reflect the older, higher figure. IRMAA determinations can be appealed.

If Social Security Administration concludes from your tax return that you owe IRMAA, you'll receive a notice with the decision and new premium amount. If that decision relies on outdated information, or you've experienced a qualifying life-changing event that permanently reduced your income, you can request a new determination with documentation — a more recent tax return, an employer letter, evidence of the life event. Qualifying events typically include marriage, divorce, death of a spouse, work stoppage or reduction, loss of income-producing property, and certain pension reductions. A year of unusually high capital gains or a one-time voluntary distribution generally won't qualify — those were choices, not life changes. But if your circumstances genuinely shifted in a way the rules recognize, you don't have to wait two years for the lookback system to catch up.

Appeals require organization: keep copies of tax returns, notices received, and documentation related to job changes or family events. There are deadlines, and sometimes more than one level of review. The process can feel bureaucratic, but it can yield meaningful savings.

7.3 Coordinating Income Flows to Protect Benefits

Ultimately, IRMAA and other means-tested costs aren't separate from your retirement plan — they're woven into it. Every withdrawal decision, every gain or loss you realize, every benefit-start decision affects both your tax bill and your Medicare costs simultaneously.

Balancing Withdrawal Sources to Control MAGI

A thoughtful withdrawal strategy is one of your most effective tools here. Instead of simply "living off the IRA" or "spending taxable accounts first," blend withdrawals across buckets to produce the income you need while keeping MAGI in a desirable range — the same sequencing logic from Chapter 4, now applied with IRMAA specifically in mind.

In years when taxable income would otherwise run low — before Social Security or RMDs have started — prioritize spending from taxable accounts, realize some long-term gains up to a comfortable level, or accelerate modest IRA withdrawals if doing so doesn't push you into an unfavorable bracket. In other years, deliberately keep distributions small, drawing on Roth accounts or accumulated cash for extra expenses so reported income doesn't cross an IRMAA threshold.

Combining sources is particularly powerful. Need $80,000 for living expenses, and know that pulling the full amount from your traditional IRA would push your MAGI just over an IRMAA cliff? Take $60,000 from the IRA and $20,000 from a Roth IRA instead.

You still have the cash you need, but you've shaped your taxable income to stay below the line that would trigger higher premiums.

Managing Capital Gains and Investment Sales

Capital gains and dividends flow directly into MAGI, which makes investment decisions a key IRMAA driver in their own right. A large portfolio sale or mutual fund distribution in a single year can be enough to push you across a cliff, especially landing on top of Social Security and RMDs you're already receiving.

Tax-loss harvesting helps here too — realizing losses to offset gains lowers your MAGI relative to what it would have been otherwise. Timing matters with capital gains the same way it matters with other income: spreading a large planned sale across two years, rather than realizing it all at once, can keep you below the cliff in both years instead of crossing it in one. Similarly, realizing gains in a year when other income is unusually low — before Social Security and RMDs begin, for instance — beats waiting until your baseline MAGI is already higher. Year-end mutual fund distributions deserve their own caution here, since they're sometimes large and not fully under your control; monitoring expected distributions and adjusting holdings before record dates, if necessary, helps you avoid an unpleasant surprise.

Coordinating RMDs and Other Income

RMDs are unavoidable once you reach the applicable age, but how you plan for them substantially influences your Medicare costs. Well before your first RMD, project what those distributions are likely to be and how they'll interact with your other income. If you see RMDs pushing your MAGI into an IRMAA tier for many years running, reducing the size of your tax-deferred accounts through Roth conversions or systematic withdrawals in your sixties shrinks both the RMDs themselves and the required income Medicare will eventually count.

Once RMDs begin, coordination becomes a year-by-year exercise. If your RMD alone brings you near a threshold, keep other taxable income minimal that year — delay elective gains or large withdrawals, cover extra spending from Roth or cash instead. If your RMD sits well below the threshold and you know future RMDs will grow, use the available headroom now to convert a bit more or realize additional gains at manageable cost.

One often-overlooked tool: the Qualified Charitable Distribution. If you're charitably inclined and 70½ or older, directing IRA money straight to a qualified charity counts toward your RMD but is excluded from income entirely — it never touches MAGI, so it doesn't affect IRMAA either. Compared to taking the RMD into your account and donating afterward, a QCD keeps both your reported income and your Medicare cost exposure lower. RMDs from inherited retirement accounts count toward MAGI too, so a comprehensive view across all your required distributions — not just your own primary accounts — is essential.

Using Spousal Income Coordination

For married couples filing jointly, IRMAA thresholds are based on combined MAGI, not each spouse's income separately — both a challenge and an opportunity. A large withdrawal or conversion by one spouse can push the couple's joint income over a threshold even if the other spouse has little or no income of their own. At the same time, thoughtful coordination lets a couple distribute income more evenly over time, reducing the chance of abrupt jumps.

Start with a joint income map covering both spouses' retirement accounts, Social Security benefits, pensions, and any ongoing work. Consider the ages each spouse will claim Social Security and begin RMDs — it may make sense for one spouse to delay claiming longer than the other, or to emphasize Roth conversions in one spouse's accounts earlier, depending on their respective balances and ages. If one spouse continues working part-time, the other might take smaller IRA distributions that year, shifting more withdrawals to a later year when joint income is lower. If both spouses hold traditional IRAs, conversions can be spread between the two to avoid concentrating all the conversion income in a single account in a single year.

Survivorship deserves its own attention here. When one spouse dies, the survivor typically moves from filing jointly to filing single, with lower IRMAA thresholds — even though many income sources, like the survivor's own Social Security and retirement accounts, remain similar. Planning while both spouses are alive to reduce future RMDs and build Roth balances can protect the surviving spouse from being pushed into higher IRMAA brackets later, once the wider joint thresholds are no longer available.

A pattern runs through this entire chapter: IRMAA and other means-tested costs aren't random penalties. They're predictable consequences of your income footprint over time. Combine what you already know about tax-efficient withdrawals, Social Security timing, and RMD management with the specific rules around Medicare premiums, and you can design a retirement income strategy that keeps more of your money working for you instead of disappearing into unexpected surcharges.

Key Takeaways

• IRMAA is calculated from your MAGI two years prior — a 2026 income decision affects your 2028 Medicare premium

• IRMAA works on a strict cliff basis: one dollar over a threshold triggers the full surcharge for the entire year, with no gradual phase-in

• Roth conversions, even though tax-free on withdrawal, still count toward MAGI in the year of conversion — visible to IRMAA even though future withdrawals won't be

• Qualified Roth withdrawals, HSA withdrawals for medical expenses, and return of principal from a taxable account do not count toward MAGI — useful levers for staying under a threshold

• For married couples, IRMAA is based on combined household MAGI, not each spouse's income separately

• IRMAA determinations can be appealed following a genuine life-changing event — marriage, divorce, death of a spouse, or work stoppage — without waiting for the two-year lookback to self-correct

Chapter 8: Annuities, Life Insurance, and Insurance Alternatives Explained

Chapter at a Glance

What you'll learn in this chapter:

• The real differences between fixed, variable, and immediate annuities — and how each is taxed

• How non-qualified annuity payouts split into taxable and tax-free portions through the exclusion ratio

• What cash-value life insurance actually offers as a retirement tool, and where the costs hide

• A clear framework for deciding when insurance products earn a place in your plan, and when a simpler approach wins

Estimated reading time: 32 minutes

> ***FIELD NOTE*** *Insurance products get sold with confidence and explained with jargon, which makes them hard to evaluate on your own terms. Nothing in this chapter is anti-annuity or anti-insurance — some of these tools genuinely fit certain situations. The goal is just to get you to the point where you're choosing rather than being chosen for.*

If you've ever sat across from an advisor and felt your eyes glaze over as they started explaining annuities, riders, cash-value life insurance, and "tax-deferred accumulation," you're not alone. Insurance-based retirement products live in a strange space — marketed like investments, regulated like insurance, taxed by rules that feel like their own private language. Yet these tools can play a real role in a retirement tax strategy, if you understand what they're actually doing for you, what they cost, and how the tax rules work.

This chapter explores annuities and life insurance as potential retirement income tools, then compares them to straightforward investment strategies. By the end, you'll see where these products genuinely fit, where they clearly don't, and how to evaluate them with a cool head instead of a sales pitch doing the thinking for you. You don't need to become an insurance actuary — you need one honest framework: what problem am I solving, what am I giving up to solve it this way, and how are taxes affected now and later?

8.1 Pros and Cons of Annuities and How They Are Taxed

Annuities are fundamentally contracts with an insurance company. You give the insurer money — a lump sum or a series of payments — and in return get tax-deferred growth, future income, or both. The core idea: trade a pile of money for a stream of income you cannot outlive. The complexity comes from the many variations on that theme.

Types of Annuities

Three broad categories cover most situations. A fixed annuity works much like a CD issued by an insurer instead of a bank — a stated interest rate, often guaranteed for three to seven years, with principal protected as long as you meet the contract terms. That stability appeals to conservative investors, though the rate may not keep pace with inflation or long-term stock returns.

A variable annuity links your returns to underlying investment "subaccounts" — stock funds, bond funds, balanced funds — so your value rises and falls with the market. This introduces real growth potential alongside real market risk; unlike a fixed annuity, there's no guarantee your value won't decline. Variable annuities often include optional riders, for an extra fee, guaranteeing minimum income or death benefits regardless of market performance — attractive, but another layer of complexity and cost.

An immediate annuity differs in timing rather than structure: you pay a single premium, often at or near retirement, and the insurer starts paying income almost immediately, usually within twelve months. Think of it as turning on a pension you create for yourself — lifetime payout, a fixed period, or a combination like "life with ten years certain." Once purchased, you typically cannot get the lump sum back; in exchange, you gain predictable cash flow for essential expenses.

Fixed and immediate annuities tend toward predictable but less flexible; variable annuities offer more upside with more risk and typically higher ongoing fees. An immediate annuity trades control over principal for guaranteed income; deferred fixed or variable annuities keep more control during accumulation but carry surrender charges and tax rules at withdrawal.

Benefits of Annuities for Retirement Income

The core strength of an annuity is guaranteed income, sometimes for life — directly addressing one of the biggest retirement fears, outliving your savings. By pooling longevity risk across many policyholders, insurers can offer income that's hard to replicate on your own without either overspending or underspending. Having a portion of expenses covered by guaranteed income, whether Social Security, a pension, or an annuity, can reduce the stress of market volatility: if essential bills are covered regardless of what markets do, you may feel freer to invest the rest of your portfolio for growth.

Annuities also offer tax-deferred growth — earnings aren't taxed annually as interest, dividends, or gains, so they compound without current tax friction until withdrawal. The catch: unlike long-term capital gains in a brokerage account, annuity earnings are eventually taxed as ordinary income, not preferential capital gains rates. The deferral is a timing advantage, not a rate advantage. Optional riders can add guaranteed lifetime withdrawal benefits, long-term care riders, or enhanced death benefits — versatile, but every rider has a cost, stacking on top of already substantial base fees.

Drawbacks and Costs to Consider

The downsides matter as much as the benefits. Cost tops the list — annuities, especially variable ones, often carry multiple fee layers: mortality and expense charges, administrative fees, underlying fund management fees, rider charges. Individually small, together they can easily exceed 2% a year, and over a long retirement horizon, that erodes returns substantially compared to low-cost investment accounts.

Liquidity is the second issue. Most deferred annuities impose surrender charges on withdrawals beyond a limited percentage during the early contract years — commonly seven to ten years, with penalties highest early and declining over time. Withdraw large amounts even after surrender charges expire, and you can still trigger taxes and, under 59½, potential penalties. Complexity works against consumers too: dense contract language, riders that dramatically change behavior and cost, sales presentations that emphasize guarantees while downplaying restrictions. And there's a real opportunity cost — money in an annuity isn't available for flexible taxable investing or opportunistic Roth conversions that might fit your broader tax plan better.

Taxation of Annuity Income

Non-qualified annuities — funded with after-tax dollars outside an IRA or employer plan — have already-taxed principal. Earnings grow tax-deferred, and at withdrawal, the IRS taxes the earnings portion as ordinary income while treating your original basis as a tax-free return of capital. For annuitized non-qualified contracts, an "exclusion ratio" splits each payment between return-of-basis and earnings, so you're never taxed twice on the same dollars — once your full basis is returned, every subsequent payment becomes fully taxable.

Fund an annuity inside a qualified plan or IRA instead, and contributions are generally pre-tax — both principal and earnings were untaxed going in, so essentially all distributions are ordinary income coming out. A "qualified annuity" is really just another form of tax-deferred retirement account; only the payout structure differs from the basic tax rules you already know.

Withdrawal ordering matters too. Non-annuitized withdrawals from non-qualified annuities use a "last-in, first-out" approach — gains come out first, fully taxable, before you begin recovering basis tax-free. Under 59½, those taxable withdrawals can also trigger a 10% penalty on the earnings portion, similar to early IRA distributions, making premature use of annuity funds particularly expensive. Annuitizing changes the mechanics: instead of LIFO, the exclusion ratio spreads basis over your expected payment period, taxing only part of each payment — simpler reporting, predictable after-tax income, but you lose the flexibility to change your mind and take a lump sum later. Either way, consider how annuity income will stack with Social Security, RMDs, and your other income sources to avoid unintentional bracket creep.

8.2 Life Insurance Retirement Tools and Tax Implications

Life insurance exists primarily to protect people who depend on you financially. But certain types – those that build cash value – can also serve as long-term savings vehicles with their own tax characteristics. Some advisors market these as "tax-free retirement" tools. There's some truth to that, alongside plenty of nuance.

Types of Cash-Value Life Insurance

Three categories dominate. Whole life insurance offers fixed premiums, a guaranteed death benefit, and a guaranteed minimum cash-value growth rate. Insurers may also pay dividends, usable to increase cash value, buy additional coverage, reduce premiums, or take in cash. The guarantees make it conservative – stability and predictability, but at higher premiums than term life and modest cash-value growth compared to market investments.

Universal life introduces flexibility – premiums can vary within limits, and the cash value typically earns interest based on a rate the insurer declares or ties to a benchmark. Appealing if your income is irregular, but it requires more ongoing monitoring, since underfunding can cause a lapse, especially later in life as the internal cost of insurance rises.

Variable universal life combines universal life's premium flexibility with investment choices similar to a variable annuity – cash value invested in separate accounts that can grow or shrink with the market. This can build more cash value than whole or universal life in favorable conditions, but exposes you to losses, higher internal fees, and more complex monitoring. Across all three types, the underlying cost of insurance and the death benefit's role must stay central to your evaluation – these are insurance products first, and their costs and guarantees reflect that purpose.

Accessing Cash Value: Withdrawals and Loans

There are two main mechanisms for accessing cash value: partial withdrawals and policy loans. Withdrawals reduce cash value (and often the death benefit) by the amount taken. Tax rules generally let you withdraw up to your basis — total premiums paid, minus prior withdrawals — without income tax; amounts beyond basis are typically taxable, since they represent earnings. Pay $150,000 in premiums with a policy now worth $220,000, and you could usually withdraw $150,000 tax-free, with anything above that taxable.

Policy loans are different — you're technically borrowing from the insurer with the policy as collateral, and the insurer charges interest. As long as the policy stays in force and doesn't become a modified endowment contract, policy loans themselves are generally not taxable, which lets people access cash value “tax-free” in practice even though the underlying growth was never taxed. But loans aren't free money: unpaid interest compounds and can eventually cause the policy to lapse or the death benefit to shrink sharply. If the policy lapses or is surrendered with an outstanding loan, the IRS treats the unpaid balance as a distribution, with any earnings portion becoming taxable income at that point — a potentially large, unexpected tax bill. Using cash value as a retirement income source works best when it's planned, monitored, and coordinated with your other income strategies, with real attention to basis, projected loan balances, and the effect on your long-term death benefit.

Costs, Fees, and Transparency Concerns

The dual-purpose nature of these policies can obscure a simpler fact: they're expensive relative to many alternative ways of investing for retirement. Premiums themselves often run well above what the same death benefit would cost in a term policy — part of each premium covers the pure cost of insurance, part builds cash value, and part covers fees and commissions. Variable policies add underlying investment management fees on top, much like mutual funds.

Over time, these costs can materially slow cash-value growth, especially early on when surrender charges are high and much of your premium covers acquisition costs — it's common for policies to show low or even negative cash surrender value in the first several years. Policy illustrations often present optimistic projections that may understate how rising internal insurance costs as you age, or lower-than-expected returns, affect the outcome. Before committing to any cash-value policy as a retirement tool, get clear on the surrender schedule, the internal rate of return on cash value under conservative assumptions, the full fee structure, and how fragile the policy is if your circumstances change.

Tax Treatment of Death Benefits and Income

One enduring strength of life insurance: the death benefit paid to beneficiaries is generally income tax-free, making it a powerful estate and legacy tool — providing liquidity for heirs, replacing income, or balancing uneven inheritances. But treating life insurance primarily as a retirement income tool layers the tax picture. Surrenders and withdrawals can trigger taxable income if they exceed basis, and policy loans that contribute to a later lapse can create unexpectedly large taxable events.

Watch for the modified endowment contract (MEC) trap: pay too much premium relative to the death benefit within a certain time frame, and the policy can lose its favorable first-in-first-out tax treatment and become a MEC, where withdrawals and loans are taxed last-in-first-out like annuities — earnings come out first and taxable, with a possible penalty before 59½. That undermines the core appeal of tax-advantaged access, which is exactly why policy design and ongoing monitoring matter when retirement income is part of the goal. Drawing heavily on cash value during retirement reduces the death benefit — fine if your priority has shifted from legacy to lifestyle, but worth deciding deliberately rather than by default.

8.3 Insurance vs. Investment-Focused Strategies

By now you've seen that annuities and cash-value life insurance bring real benefits — guarantees, tax deferral, tax-advantaged access — at the price of higher fees, complexity, and reduced flexibility. Deciding whether they belong in your plan means comparing them directly with more straightforward investment approaches.

Differing Objectives: Protection vs. Growth

Insurance products are built around protection — annuities against longevity and sometimes market risk, life insurance against the financial consequences of your death. They transfer certain risks from you to the insurer in exchange for premiums and contractual limits. Investment accounts focus on growth and liquidity instead, offering direct exposure to stocks, bonds, and other assets without promising income you cannot outlive or a guaranteed lump sum at death. Over the long term, diversified low-cost portfolios have often delivered higher expected returns than many insurance products, especially after fees.

Neither category is universally "better" — they serve different roles, and a balanced plan often uses both. Social Security, perhaps a small immediate annuity, and a pension can secure a floor of guaranteed income for core living expenses; above that floor, a diversified investment portfolio pursues growth, handles irregular large expenses, and provides legacy potential. The right mix depends on risk tolerance, health, family situation, and your psychological comfort with market swings.

Tax Considerations Across Strategies

Investment accounts generate taxable events that can often be controlled and optimized — long-term gains and qualified dividends at preferential rates, losses harvested to offset gains. Traditional IRAs and 401(k)s defer tax until withdrawal, then tax ordinary income; Roth accounts can offer tax-free growth and withdrawals under the right conditions.

Insurance products emphasize tax deferral and sometimes tax-free access, at the cost of higher fees. Annuity earnings are taxed as ordinary income on withdrawal, with no preferential capital gains treatment. Cash-value life insurance allows tax-deferred inside buildup, with loans often providing spending power without immediate taxable income, and death benefits generally received income tax-free.

Integrating these tools means coordinating their different tax profiles deliberately — delaying annuity income until after RMDs have begun, or using it to support spending in poor-market years rather than selling investments at a loss. Use policy loans selectively, in years when other income threatens to push you into a higher bracket or trigger additional Medicare premiums. But don't overestimate the tax advantage either: a variable annuity invested in funds similar to your taxable portfolio may deliver lower after-fee returns and tax earnings at higher ordinary rates instead of capital gains rates at withdrawal. A life insurance policy overfunded purely for cash value may tie up premiums that could have gone into a Roth account or low-cost index fund instead. Evaluate numerically — compare projected after-tax outcomes under realistic assumptions, including fees, surrender charges, and your likely tax brackets now and later.

Liquidity and Flexibility Trade-offs

Liquidity — how easily you can access money without excessive cost — is an underappreciated dimension here. Taxable investment portfolios offer high liquidity, sellable within days. Even retirement accounts, with their rules and penalties, often allow rollovers and partial withdrawals. Insurance contracts impose more friction: surrender charges on early annuity withdrawals, immediate annuities that generally cannot be unwound once purchased, cash-value life insurance that's accessible through loans but risks lapse and tax issues if mismanaged.

This matters because retirement does what life does generally: it surprises you. Healthcare expenses, support for adult children, housing changes can all call for cash on short notice. A well-built plan reserves a portion of assets in liquid, transparent vehicles — perhaps a modest slice in an income annuity to secure essential spending, with the majority kept accessible in diversified investments; or a life insurance policy held primarily for legacy and risk protection, with cash value treated as a secondary or emergency resource rather than a primary paycheck.

Suitability and Fees: What's Right for You?

Insurance-based solutions can be particularly appropriate if you're deeply concerned about outliving your money and place real value on guaranteed income, lack a traditional pension and want a pension-like stream for basic expenses, want to provide for heirs through a tax-free death benefit, or have already maxed out other tax-advantaged accounts and still have assets you want to shelter and structure.

A more straightforward investment-focused approach may suit you better if you're comfortable with market risk and willing to manage an adjustable withdrawal strategy, value transparency and low cost, want maximum flexibility to change course as laws or circumstances shift, or have limited resources and need to keep expenses as low as possible to stretch your savings.

In every case, scrutinize the fee structure carefully — high ongoing costs are one of the most powerful drags on long-term wealth, especially layered on top of conservative returns. Before purchasing any annuity or cash-value policy, request detailed illustrations and disclosures: What is the mortality and expense charge? What are the underlying fund fees? How long is the surrender period and what are the charges in each year? How do riders affect cost and benefits? How does this compare, after fees and taxes, with a combination of low-cost investments and simpler insurance? Because commissions and sales incentives are common in this space, independent fee-only advice can be genuinely valuable here. Whether you work with an advisor or evaluate options yourself, the guiding principle is the same as everywhere else in this book: start with your plan, then choose products to support it — not the other way around.

Key Takeaways

- Annuity earnings are taxed as ordinary income on withdrawal, never at preferential capital gains rates — the tax deferral is a timing advantage, not a rate advantage
- Non-qualified annuity payments use an “exclusion ratio” to split each payment between tax-free return of basis and taxable earnings

• Annuity fees, particularly on variable annuities, can exceed 2% a year once mortality, expense, administrative, and rider charges are stacked together

• Cash-value life insurance lets you withdraw up to your basis tax-free; amounts beyond basis are taxable, and policy loans are generally not taxable unless the policy lapses or becomes a Modified Endowment Contract

• A life insurance death benefit is generally income tax-free, making it a genuinely useful estate and legacy tool independent of its use as a retirement income source

• Before buying any annuity or cash-value policy, get the surrender schedule, all underlying fees, and a realistic after-tax comparison against a simple low-cost investment alternative in writing

Chapter 9: Advanced Strategies: Backdoor Roths, Qualified Charitable Distributions, and Tax-Planning Tweaks

Chapter at a Glance

What you'll learn in this chapter:

• How a backdoor Roth contribution works for high earners locked out of direct contributions — and the pro-rata trap that catches people off guard

• The mechanics of Qualified Charitable Distributions, including the limitations and common reporting mistakes

• How "bunching" charitable donations and using a donor-advised fund can restore a tax benefit the standard deduction otherwise erases

• How to pair a Roth conversion year with a charitable bunching year for maximum effect

Estimated reading time: 26 minutes

> ***FIELD NOTE*** *Most of the mistakes in this chapter aren't strategic — they're paperwork mistakes. A backdoor Roth done flawlessly in spirit but reported wrong on Form 8606. A QCD that technically qualifies but never gets flagged on the return, so the IRS taxes the whole distribution anyway. The strategies here are simple. The execution is where people lose money.*

Many retirees reach a point where the basics — filling lower brackets, coordinating Social Security, managing RMDs — aren't enough anymore. The nest egg has grown, income sources have multiplied, and the tax code starts to feel like both a puzzle and a moving target. At this stage, the goal shifts from "paying what you owe" to "intentionally shaping when and how you owe it," using tools the law already provides.

This chapter covers three families of advanced strategy: backdoor Roth contributions, Qualified Charitable Distributions, and a set of tax-planning tweaks involving charitable bunching, donor-advised funds, and coordinating Roth conversions with giving. None of these require you to be a tax expert, but they do demand attention, good recordkeeping, and ideally a tax professional in your corner. The theme throughout is multi-year coordination — fitting contributions, withdrawals, and gifts together so the whole picture works better than any single decision on its own.

9.1 Backdoor Roth Contributions and Limitations

Roth IRAs offer something genuinely valuable: tax-free growth, tax-free qualified withdrawals, and no lifetime RMDs for the original owner. But they also come with income limits on direct contributions, which locks out many high earners just when they have the most disposable income to save.

The backdoor Roth is a workaround using two separate rules. Anyone with earned income can contribute to a traditional IRA regardless of income; anyone can convert traditional IRA assets to a Roth, with no income limit on conversions at all. Stitch them together: make a nondeductible contribution to a traditional IRA, then convert that contribution to a Roth.

Understanding the Purpose

The goal is letting high-income retirees and pre-retirees continue building Roth assets despite the front-door income limits. For someone still earning consulting income or part-time wages and ineligible for direct Roth contributions, routing an after-tax contribution through a traditional IRA and converting recreates the effect of a direct Roth contribution — after-tax money ends up in a Roth, where future growth and qualified withdrawals are tax-free.

Regularly adding even modest amounts via the backdoor steadily increases your pool of tax-free dollars. A larger Roth bucket gives more flexibility later — tapping it in years when other income spikes, or preserving it as a tax-advantaged legacy for heirs. This is less about a one-time windfall and more about steadily improving your long-run tax position.

Step-by-Step Process

The mechanics are simple in concept, but execution matters. Establish a traditional IRA if you don't already have one — ideally at the same custodian as your Roth IRA, which simplifies the transfer. Contribute nondeductible funds: you don't claim a deduction, since you're using after-tax dollars, and traditional IRAs have no income limit on contributions, only on deductibility, so high earners can contribute even without a deduction.

Once the contribution settles — usually a day or two — convert the full amount to your Roth IRA. Many people hold the contribution in cash or a money market fund during this window to minimize any taxable gain between contribution and conversion; converting promptly keeps any such gains very small. Converting the full balance, rather than leaving a small after-tax residue, also avoids complicating future pro-rata calculations.

The critical final step happens at tax time: report the nondeductible contribution and the conversion correctly on IRS Form 8606. This form tracks your after-tax basis in traditional IRAs and ensures you're not taxed again on money you already paid tax on going in. Most backdoor Roth problems trace back to an incomplete or incorrect Form 8606 — worth coordinating with a tax professional, at least the first time you do this.

The Pro-Rata Rule

If a backdoor Roth only ever involved a brand-new, empty traditional IRA, it would be straightforward. The complication is the IRS pro-rata rule: when you convert money from any traditional IRA to a Roth, the IRS looks at all your traditional, SEP, and SIMPLE IRAs combined — not just the account you're converting from.

Say you have $93,000 of pre-tax money across various traditional IRAs, and this year you make a $7,500 nondeductible contribution intending a backdoor Roth. Your total IRA balance is now $100,500, of which $7,500 is after-tax basis. Convert that $7,500, and you might hope all of it comes out tax-free. The pro-rata rule prevents that: only about 7.5% of any conversion counts as after-tax, and the rest is taxable. In dollar terms, that conversion yields roughly $560 tax-free and $6,940 of taxable income. You don't get to choose which dollars you're converting — every conversion is treated as a proportional mix of pre-tax and after-tax money. This rule catches people off guard constantly, especially those who rolled an old 401(k) into a traditional IRA without realizing they were setting up this exact constraint.

The calculation uses your total end-of-year IRA balance, not the balance on conversion day — meaning a last-minute rollover into or out of an IRA late in the year can shift your pro-rata percentage. If you want to clean up your situation, perhaps by rolling pre-tax IRA money into a current 401(k) to isolate your after-tax basis, leave time for that transfer to settle before December 31. Before pursuing a backdoor Roth, inventory every IRA you hold — traditional, rollover, SEP, SIMPLE — and identify how much of each is pre-tax versus after-tax basis tracked on past Forms 8606. Only with the full picture can you estimate the real tax cost of a conversion and decide whether to proceed, adjust, or look for an alternative.

Limitations and Potential Pitfalls

The backdoor Roth isn't universally appropriate. With significant pre-tax IRA balances and no access to a plan that accepts roll-ins, the pro-rata rule can make the strategy costly — paying ordinary tax on most of a small conversion each year may not be worth the incremental Roth assets gained.

Age and timing matter too: you can convert at any age, but accessing converted funds too early triggers penalties. Withdrawing converted amounts penalty-free generally requires being at least 59½ and meeting a five-year holding period for each conversion. There's also a lingering legal question — the "step transaction doctrine" — around whether contributing and converting almost immediately could theoretically be challenged as circumventing Roth income limits. The IRS hasn't specifically barred backdoor Roths, and they remain widely used, but some advisors suggest waiting a short period between contribution and conversion to keep the steps clearly distinct; others prioritize minimizing taxable gains and convert quickly. There's no single right answer, just an awareness that some uncertainty exists.

Once converted, you can't undo it — recharacterizations are no longer allowed. If your income later falls dramatically, you can't "unconvert," which is exactly why projecting your likely current versus future bracket matters before you act. And tax law evolves: proposals periodically surface in Congress to curtail backdoor Roths or limit after-tax conversions. Revisit your plan annually, and don't treat any single strategy as the linchpin of your retirement.

9.2 Qualified Charitable Distributions to Reduce Taxable Income

As retirees age into their seventies and beyond, RMDs often become the primary driver of taxable income — money you must withdraw and pay ordinary tax on, whether you need it or not. For charitably inclined retirees, this is frustrating: you may already be giving regularly, but writing checks from a taxable checking account does nothing to reduce the RMD-driven income on your return. QCDs offer a direct alternative: send money straight from your IRA to a charity in a way that satisfies your RMD but never shows up as income at all.

Basics of QCDs

A QCD is a direct transfer from your IRA to a qualified charity, available once you're 70½ — a different threshold than the RMD starting age, which means there's a window where you're not yet required to take RMDs but can already use QCDs to shrink your IRA and lower future RMDs preemptively.

Once made, the distribution counts toward your RMD for the year but is excluded from AGI entirely. This is meaningfully different from taking the distribution as income and then claiming a deduction for the donation: in the deduction route, income rises first and a deduction brings it back down; with a QCD, income never rises in the first place. Because QCDs bypass AGI, the benefit ripples beyond the immediate tax savings — into Social Security taxation, eligibility for certain credits, and Medicare IRMAA exposure, all of which key off AGI or MAGI. QCDs also work even if you take the standard deduction, which most retirees do since the 2017 tax law changes —

writing a personal check provides no federal benefit if you don't itemize, but a QCD restores a tax-efficient path regardless.

Using QCDs to Meet RMD Requirements

The mechanics are straightforward but detail-sensitive. You must be at least 70½ on the date the distribution leaves the IRA — turning 70½ at some point during the year isn't enough; it's measured to the day. The money must move directly from the custodian to the charity; withdrawing funds into your own account and writing a personal check afterward is just a regular taxable distribution followed by a donation, not a QCD. Many custodians will send a check payable to the charity but mailed to you for delivery — that still counts, provided the check itself is made out to the charity, not to you.

QCDs are capped at an annual maximum per person, indexed for inflation. Within that cap, every QCD dollar offsets your RMD dollar for dollar — a $30,000 RMD satisfied with $20,000 in QCDs still requires a $10,000 taxable distribution to complete it. Send more than your RMD as QCDs, and the excess (within the annual cap) still qualifies as a QCD but won't carry forward to reduce next year's RMD. Keep good records: your 1099-R will show total distributions without breaking out the QCD portion, so you need to report the full distribution and separately show how much was excluded, retaining acknowledgment letters from the charity just as you would for any other donation. And confirm eligibility before sending a large QCD — public charities recognized by the IRS qualify, but donor-advised funds, private foundations, and supporting organizations do not.

Impact on Tax Brackets and Medicare Costs

The surface benefit is avoiding tax on money you planned to give away anyway. The deeper value is in keeping your reported income lower, year after year. Near the top of a bracket while also planning a partial Roth conversion? Without QCDs, your RMD pushes part of that conversion into the next higher bracket; rerouting some or all of the RMD as QCDs drops your AGI and may preserve room to execute the conversion at the lower rate. The same logic applies to Social Security taxation — QCDs keep provisional income lower, reducing how much of your benefit gets taxed — and to IRMAA, where keeping

AGI below key thresholds can save hundreds or thousands a year in Medicare premiums. The point isn't that QCDs always beat taking a distribution and itemizing — it's that they're one part of a coordinated income plan, working alongside Roth conversions, gain harvesting, and the timing of other income to produce a smoother overall tax profile.

Limitations and Common Mistakes

A few recurring errors trip people up. QCDs can only come from IRAs — typically traditional, sometimes inherited, subject to specific rules — never directly from an employer plan like a 401(k); rolling a portion into an IRA first is the workaround if your money is still inside an employer plan. The receiving organization matters too: donor-advised funds and private non-operating foundations don't qualify, and people who give regularly through a DAF sometimes mistakenly assume they can replenish it with QCDs.

Timing mistakes are common as well — take your full RMD as a regular distribution early in the year, then decide to do a QCD later, and the QCD still excludes income but won't retroactively reduce the RMD you already satisfied. For maximum benefit, process QCDs before or in place of other IRA distributions, not after. On the reporting side, failing to designate part of the distribution as a QCD on the return means the IRS treats the full amount as taxable, quietly erasing the benefit — correctable with an amended return, but better to get it right the first time. And remember that QCDs use up IRA dollars that might otherwise be converted to Roth or left for heirs — if you have both large charitable goals and a desire to leave money to family, you may face real trade-offs in deciding whether to give from IRAs during life via QCDs, leave IRAs to charity at death, or preserve IRA balances for heirs and give from other accounts instead. For 2026, the annual maximum that can be excluded from income via QCD is $111,000 per person, subject to future inflation adjustments — worth verifying against the current-year figure each time you plan, since this number moves.

9.3 Tax-Efficient Charitable Giving and Deduction "Bunching"

Beyond QCDs, retirees who give regularly have additional tools for shaping when their gifts produce a tax benefit. The central challenge: the standard deduction has grown large enough that many households no longer itemize at all. If your total itemized deductions — charitable gifts, mortgage interest, state and local taxes — fall below the standard deduction, your giving may be generous but tax-invisible.

That gap got wider in 2025. A new deduction — $6,000 per person, on top of the regular standard deduction and the existing extra amount for filers 65 and older — now applies to anyone 65+ through the 2028 tax year, regardless of whether they itemize. A married couple where both spouses qualify gets $12,000 combined. It phases out gradually above $75,000 of MAGI for single filers and $150,000 for joint filers, fully disappearing at $175,000 and $350,000. For most retirees under those thresholds, it pushes the standard deduction high enough that itemizing charitable gifts — bunched or not — clears the bar even less often than before. That doesn't make QCDs or bunching pointless; it makes QCDs more valuable by comparison, since they bypass the itemize-or-don't decision entirely.

The Concept of Bunching

Bunching means intentionally consolidating several years' worth of donations into a single tax year. Instead of $10,000 annually to various charities, give $30,000 in one year and little or nothing the year before and after. Economically, you've given the same total over three years; for tax purposes, you've created one high-deduction year and two low-deduction years. In the high-deduction year, your donations plus other itemizable expenses may exceed the standard deduction, letting you itemize and capture a real benefit; in the low-deduction years, you simply take the standard deduction. Compared to giving evenly every year, this pattern can produce more total tax savings across the period.

To make bunching effective, think ahead about both your giving and your other income. If you expect a spike in taxable income — a business sale, a large IRA distribution, a Roth conversion — aligning a bunching year with that high-income year lets the larger deduction blunt the impact, keeping you in a more favorable bracket and possibly reducing IRMAA exposure too.

Using Donor-Advised Funds

For retirees with predictable philanthropic commitments who don't want to dramatically vary what their favorite charities receive each year, a donor-advised fund solves the emotional hurdle bunching otherwise creates. A DAF is essentially a charitable investment account: you make an irrevocable contribution — cash or appreciated securities — and receive a deduction in the contribution year, subject to limits, while the DAF (sponsored by a public charity or financial institution) invests the assets and you recommend grants out to your chosen charities whenever you wish.

This is tailor-made for bunching: contribute three years' worth of anticipated donations to a DAF in one tax year, itemize that year, then have the DAF send grants to your charities on the usual schedule in subsequent years. The receiving organizations see no change in their support; your tax return shows deductions concentrated into one high-impact year. DAFs also simplify recordkeeping — your tax receipt is the DAF contribution itself, with no need for separate acknowledgments from every downstream charity — and the assets can grow inside the fund before being granted out. From an estate-planning angle, a DAF can reduce the size of a taxable estate and lets you name successors to continue recommending grants after your death. DAFs can't receive QCDs, but they fit naturally alongside QCDs, outright giving, and bequests as part of a broader charitable strategy.

Integrating Roth Conversions with Charitable Giving

Roth conversions raise taxable income in the conversion year. Adding charitable giving to the picture opens a useful possibility: in a year you're planning a sizable conversion — to take advantage of a temporarily low bracket, a market downturn, or the gap between retirement and Social Security — also bunch your charitable deductions. A large contribution to a DAF or directly to charities creates a deduction that partially offsets the conversion income.

The result can be a deliberately designed tax year: income rises through the conversion, but the effective rate stays moderate thanks to the larger deduction. Over time, you've shifted money from the tax-deferred bucket to the tax-free Roth bucket, funded several years of giving in advance, and kept control over when charities actually receive the funds. Coordinating this requires attention to AGI-based deduction limits, which differ for cash gifts versus appreciated securities and for different types of recipient organizations, plus awareness of how much additional income you can recognize before tripping a higher IRMAA tier two years later. This is where multi-year projections — income, deductions, RMDs, and conversions plotted on a timeline together — earn their keep.

Practical Steps to Implement Giving Strategies

Start by clarifying your charitable goals independent of tax considerations — which causes matter most, how much you realistically want to give over the next five to ten years. Writing down even an informal giving policy makes it easier to align tax strategy without feeling like the tax tail is wagging the dog.

Gather data on current and projected income — Social Security, pensions, annuities, part-time work, RMDs, anticipated conversions — and sketch out likely high- and low-income years, noting how close projected income comes to key tax and Medicare thresholds. Pair giving strategies with that pattern: designate certain years as bunching years tied to large conversions or asset sales, and rely more on QCDs or routine giving from taxable accounts in other years. Keep meticulous records throughout — instructions to custodians and acknowledgment letters for QCDs, contribution and grant confirmations for DAFs, dates and basis documentation for conversions.

Review the whole plan at least annually. Health changes, family events, legislative shifts, and market moves can all alter the optimal timing of conversions and gifts. Backdoor Roths, QCDs, and charitable bunching aren't about outsmarting the tax code — they're about using it as written to support the life and legacy you actually want.

Key Takeaways

• A backdoor Roth combines two separate rules — anyone can contribute (nondeductibly) to a traditional IRA, and anyone can convert to a Roth — to get money into a Roth despite income limits

• The IRS pro-rata rule looks at the combined balance of all your traditional, SEP, and SIMPLE IRAs, not just the account you're converting from — this can make a "clean" backdoor Roth costly if you hold other pre-tax IRA money

• Form 8606 is the single most common point of failure in a backdoor Roth — get this reported correctly every year

• A QCD must move directly from the IRA custodian to the charity, is capped at $111,000 per person for 2026, and only counts if processed before or in place of your regular RMD

• "Bunching" charitable donations into a single high-deduction year, often through a donor-advised fund, restores a tax benefit that the standard deduction otherwise erases for occasional itemizers

• Pairing a Roth conversion year with a charitable bunching year lets the larger deduction offset some of the conversion's tax impact

Chapter 10: Building Personalized Tools: Worksheets, Calculators, and Templates

Chapter at a Glance

What you'll learn in this chapter:

• A four-column worksheet for mapping every income source you have by its tax character

• A year-by-year withdrawal sequencing template that turns strategy into concrete numbers

• A multi-year tax bracket planner for spotting income spikes before they happen

• A Roth conversion calculator blueprint and an annual tax-planning checklist you can reuse every year

Estimated reading time: 24 minutes

> ***FIELD NOTE*** *None of the tools in this chapter require software or a finance background. A piece of paper and four columns gets you most of the way there. What they require is doing it once, then actually returning to it every year — that's the part almost everyone skips.*

Most people are used to tax season feeling like a flurry of forms and last-minute decisions. Retirement can amplify that: multiple income sources, more complicated rules, and the nagging fear that one misstep means paying more than necessary. Much of that anxiety comes from trying to juggle everything in your head. The moment you move decisions into a well-designed worksheet, planner, or checklist, your choices get clearer and easier to manage.

This chapter gives you three practical structures: a Withdrawal Sequencing Worksheet to map where each dollar of income comes from and in what order; a Multi-Year Tax Bracket Planner to see the big picture across several years instead of being surprised one year at a time; and a Roth Conversion Calculator Blueprint paired with an Annual Tax Checklist to evaluate conversions and keep your plan current as life and the tax rules change. You don't need to be "good with numbers" to use any of this — the point isn't a perfect forecast, it's making your decisions visible, testable, and repeatable.

10.1 Withdrawal Sequencing Worksheet

Understanding Your Income Sources

The first section lists every possible source of retirement income you have or expect to have. Seeing them side by side, with their tax treatment, is surprisingly clarifying. Build a simple table with four columns: Income Source, Type (Taxable, Tax-Deferred, Tax-Free, Other), Estimated Annual Amount, and Tax Treatment Notes.

Under Income Source, list everything relevant: Social Security, traditional IRA withdrawals, 401(k)/403(b) withdrawals, Roth withdrawals, pension income, annuity income, brokerage withdrawals, bank interest, rental income, HSA distributions if applicable, and any part-time or consulting income. Assign each to a category — taxable accounts (brokerage, bank interest, non-qualified annuity gains, with long-term gains and qualified dividends getting favorable treatment); tax-deferred (traditional IRAs, 401(k)s, 403(b)s, most pensions, taxed as ordinary income on withdrawal); tax-free (Roth IRAs and 401(k)s for qualified distributions, HSA withdrawals for qualified medical expenses); and "other" for items like return of basis or unusual settlements.

In the Tax Treatment Notes column, jot quick reminders that will matter later — "counts toward AGI; affects Social Security taxation and IRMAA," "long-term gains likely at 0%–15%," "Roth: qualified withdrawals tax-free, no RMDs." This exercise does two things: it makes sure you're not forgetting an account, and it forces clarity on how each dollar will actually show up on your return — essential once you start experimenting with different withdrawal orders.

Step-by-Step Sequencing Process

The core of the worksheet is a year-by-year withdrawal schedule, turning big-picture strategy into concrete numbers. Create columns for Year, Age, Social Security Income, Pension/Annuity Income,

Taxable Withdrawals, Tax-Deferred Withdrawals, Roth Withdrawals, Other Income, Total Gross Income, Estimated Taxable Income, and Notes. Fill in your best estimates for each year you want to plan — often from your planned retirement date through at least age 80.

Note where a source starts or stops: Social Security might begin at 67 or 70, a pension at a fixed age, part-time work phasing out over a few years, RMDs starting at your applicable age (currently 73 or 75 depending on birth year). Start with income you can't easily control — pensions, annuities, Social Security — then add the withdrawals you choose from taxable, tax-deferred, and Roth accounts to meet your spending target. For each year: enter your desired after-tax spending goal, subtract fixed known income, determine how much additional gross income you need from your accounts after estimated taxes, then decide which accounts to tap based on your tax strategy and goals — reducing future RMDs, preserving Roth balances, or whatever matters most that year. Use the Total Gross Income and Estimated Taxable Income columns to see how close you're tracking to the top of your current bracket. Even a rough estimate using last year's brackets is genuinely useful here.

Customizing for Individual Situations

No two retirees have the same mix of accounts, spending patterns, or goals — the worksheet should flex to match your situation rather than impose a rigid template. Add columns or notes for planned Roth conversions distinct from regular withdrawals, state tax considerations if you live in or plan to move to a state with different rules, anticipated large expenses, healthcare costs (especially before Medicare or for possible long-term care later), and changes in filing status such as the death of a spouse, which can dramatically alter brackets. A notes section documenting your assumptions — expected returns, inflation, whether you assume today's brackets hold — turns the worksheet into a planning journal rather than a one-time exercise, so when you revisit it, you can see exactly why you made last year's choices and what's changed since.

Visualizing Tax Impact

Once your withdrawal pattern is laid out by year, the final purpose is making tax impact hard to ignore. Many retirement mistakes happen because people don't realize one extra distribution will push them into a higher bracket, increase the taxable share of Social Security, or trigger an IRMAA surcharge. Build simple visual cues in: shade rows where Estimated Taxable Income crosses into a new bracket, mark years close to an IRMAA threshold, flag years with unusually low taxable income as opportunities for 0% capital gains harvesting or extra conversions at low cost. Even on paper, a star next to a "tax window" year or an exclamation mark next to a hazard makes the worksheet easy to scan for risks and opportunities at a glance. Over time, this becomes a living document — compare actual outcomes to plan each year, adjust, and extend the horizon another year or two.

10.2 Multi-Year Tax Bracket Planner and Tracker

The Withdrawal Sequencing Worksheet handles one year's mechanics at a time, even spanning multiple years. The Multi-Year Tax Bracket Planner shifts the lens: showing how your taxable income moves across years, and where you can smooth or reshape that pattern. Small choices in your sixties can change what you pay in your seventies and eighties — this planner makes that long-range view tangible.

Projecting Future Income Streams

Set up a grid with years down the left side and income categories across the top — age (yours and a spouse's), estimated Social Security, pensions and annuities, tax-deferred withdrawals or RMDs, Roth withdrawals, taxable account gains and interest, earned income, and other income like rental or royalties. Add a column for Total Projected Taxable Income and another for Tax Bracket/Marginal Rate. These don't need to be perfect — they're meant to reveal shape: is your income even year to year, or does it spike at certain ages? Are there low-income valleys worth using deliberately? Mark one-time events on the same timeline — a planned property sale, a lump-sum pension distribution or inheritance, a major Roth conversion year, a year you expect to help a child with a large expense — so they don't ambush you at tax time.

Tracking Yearly Brackets and Margins

With income estimated for each year, the next step is placing that income within the federal (and optionally state) bracket system. The key concept is your "bracket margin" — how much room remains in your current bracket before the next one. Include the top of your current marginal bracket, your projected taxable income, and the headroom between them. That headroom tells you how much room exists for Roth conversions without crossing a bracket, extra long-term gains, or accelerating tax-deferred income before RMDs grow. Overlay state brackets too if state income tax matters in your situation. You don't need exact tax calculations every time — a simplified, conservative estimate of taxable income and bracket thresholds is usually enough to reveal trends and risks.

Identifying Smoothing Opportunities

Looking down the Taxable Income column year by year, the goal isn't perfect flatness — it's avoiding unnecessary spikes: years where income jumps into a higher bracket or triggers a surcharge, followed by lean years that waste available bracket space. Common patterns include low taxable income in early retirement before Social Security and RMDs begin, sharp increases once both kick in together, and bumps tied to one-time sales or distributions. Where you see big differences between years, ask whether income could shift from a high year into a low one through earlier withdrawals, or the reverse if you expect future brackets to rise, and whether there are partial-conversion opportunities in the valley years. Comparing income across years this way lets you design a more even pattern — not eliminating all variability, but deliberately avoiding the highs and lows that cost you in taxes or Medicare premiums.

A Worked Example

Imagine you're 62, planning to retire at 65, and intend to start Social Security at 70. A first pass at the planner might show ages 65–69 with no Social Security, moderate tax-deferred withdrawals, and spending partly from taxable accounts; ages 70–72 with Social Security plus gradually increasing tax-deferred withdrawals; and 73 onward with full RMDs and Social Security both fully in play. The process: pick a planning horizon (say, 60 to 85), fill in known or highly likely income by year, add estimated tax-deferred withdrawals to meet spending before RMDs, layer in RMD estimates beginning at your required age, see how taxable income moves and mark the high- and low-income years, then experiment with adjustments — shifting some withdrawals earlier, for instance — to smooth the pattern and open up Roth conversion windows. The goal isn't guessing the future perfectly. It's a map you can revise, track, and refine so you're always looking several years ahead when making this year's decisions.

10.3 Roth Conversion Calculator Blueprint and Annual Tax Checklist

Roth conversions are one of the few levers in retirement that let you deliberately move income from one year to another. Done thoughtfully, they reduce your lifetime tax bill, manage RMDs, and increase future flexibility. Done carelessly, they trigger large tax bills, raise Medicare premiums, or push more Social Security into the taxable zone.

Blueprint for Calculating Conversion Tax Impact

A useful conversion calculator doesn't need to be complex. At its core, it answers three questions: how much additional tax will I owe this year if I convert a given amount, how does that affect my marginal rate (and possibly IRMAA), and what's the potential long-term benefit of moving those dollars into a tax-free environment?

Build one with these inputs: current-year projected taxable income without conversions, the desired conversion amount, current-year bracket thresholds (federal and state, if applicable), your expected marginal rate this year, a rough assumption for future rates, and a growth rate assumption for the converted funds. The calculator estimates how much of the conversion falls into your current bracket versus spilling into the next. If your projected taxable income is $70,000, the top of your current bracket is $95,000, and you convert $20,000, the first $25,000 of room absorbs the entire conversion at your current rate. Convert $40,000 under the same conditions instead, and $25,000 stays in your current bracket while $15,000 gets taxed at the next bracket's rate. Multiply each slice by its marginal rate to estimate the immediate tax due, then extend the same logic to approximate IRMAA impact against the thresholds from Chapter 7. To capture the potential long-term benefit, simulate what happens if the same amount stayed in the tax-deferred account and got withdrawn later instead — a straight-line comparison, same growth rate in both accounts with a future tax rate applied to the deferred scenario, gives you a sense of whether paying tax now is likely to pay off. This blueprint isn't about perfect forecasts. It's a consistent way to test different conversion sizes within each year's tax window and compare them against your multi-year plan.

Evaluating Conversion Timing and Amount

Once you can estimate the cost, the next question is how much and when — this is where the Withdrawal Sequencing Worksheet and the Multi-Year Planner connect directly to the calculator. Use the planner to find years with relatively low projected taxable income — often early retirement, before RMDs and full Social Security — where bracket margins allow meaningful conversions at lower rates. Then run scenarios: convert up to the top of your current bracket, or only to a lower personally acceptable limit, or compare a single large conversion against several smaller staggered ones. The goal is balance — converting enough to meaningfully reduce future RMDs and build a tax-free pool, without converting so much in any one year that you regret the tax or surcharge consequences. Revisit this whenever life changes — an early retirement, a large investment gain, a move to a different tax state, a shift in family situation — since any of these can flip whether a given year is a good conversion year. The calculator and planner give you a quick way to test the new situation before deciding.

Annual Retirement Tax Planning Checklist

Even the best tools only help if used consistently. A concise yearly checklist makes that manageable:

• Review last year's actual income from all sources and compare it with your plan

• Update your Withdrawal Sequencing Worksheet and Multi-Year Planner with new balances, projections, and life changes

• Check current-year tax bracket thresholds and standard deduction amounts

• Estimate this year's taxable income, including fixed sources and planned withdrawals

• Identify how much room remains in your current bracket and whether there's an opportunity for conversions or harvesting long-term gains at favorable rates

• Review your RMD status and confirm you have a strategy for satisfying it without unnecessary bracket jumps

• Consider Medicare IRMAA implications if you're near a threshold

• Revisit charitable giving, including any QCD opportunities if you're eligible

• Confirm your investment allocation is still appropriate after withdrawals and market movement, and rebalance in a tax-aware way

• Note any expected changes next year — a spouse claiming Social Security, a planned downsizing sale, a pension start date — that might call for action this year instead

Treat this like a yearly health exam for your retirement tax plan. Once the tools are set up, it shouldn't take much time, and the real value comes from catching problems before they become costly surprises, and deliberately using temporary opportunities while they're open.

Tips for Incorporating New Tax Rules and Life Changes

Any planning system needs to be robust to change. Tax laws evolve, thresholds get indexed to inflation, and occasionally a major reform reshapes brackets or account rules entirely. A few habits help: refresh your tax assumptions once a year after updated brackets are published; re-run your projections whenever a significant life event occurs — a retirement date change, a major health development, a move to a new state, an inheritance, the loss of a spouse; keep a simple journal attached to your planner noting unexpected outcomes, like a conversion that triggered a bigger IRMAA hit than you expected, since these are valuable data for refining your approach next time; and periodically check your overall strategy against current expert discussion, not to chase every new idea, but to stay aware of major shifts like changing RMD ages or new Roth rules.

Build these habits into your annual checklist, and your worksheet, planner, and calculator stop being static templates you filled in once and become living tools you actually consult and update. The goal across this entire book has never been to outsmart the tax code in one heroic maneuver — it's to make a series of thoughtful, informed decisions, year after year, that keep your income sustainable, your taxes reasonable, and your stress level low.

Key Takeaways

• A four-column income worksheet (Source, Type, Amount, Tax Treatment Notes) is the fastest way to see your full tax picture at a glance

• A year-by-year withdrawal sequencing table turns abstract strategy into concrete numbers you can actually act on each December

• A multi-year tax bracket planner reveals income spikes — like RMDs and Social Security arriving in the same years — well before they happen

- A simple Roth conversion calculator needs only a few inputs: current bracket position, conversion amount, and a rough future-rate assumption
- An annual checklist — reviewing brackets, RMD status, IRMAA proximity, and charitable opportunities — turns a one-time plan into a living system
- None of these tools require software; a notebook or basic spreadsheet is enough to get real value from all three

Chapter 11: Case Studies and Step-by-Step Scenarios

Chapter at a Glance

What you'll learn in this chapter:

• How filing status alone — single versus married filing jointly — can change the tax outcome of an identical withdrawal

• A side-by-side comparison of a conservative, bond-heavy retiree and a growth-focused, equity-heavy retiree facing very different tax challenges

• How a couple converting $40,000-$60,000 a year compares to a single filer converting $10,000-$15,000 a year, and why the gap exists

• Real IRMAA scenarios showing how a home renovation, a Roth conversion, and a spouse's death each ripple into Medicare premiums two years later

Estimated reading time: 31 minutes

> ***FIELD NOTE*** *Every strategy in this book sounds reasonable in the abstract. What changes people's minds is seeing the actual dollar figures move when one variable changes — filing status, portfolio style, the year a sale happens. This chapter is built entirely out of those moments.*

Understanding retirement tax strategy in theory is useful, but most people don't really feel the impact until they see numbers on a page. Abstract ideas like "bracket management" or "Roth conversion windows" sound technical and distant, until a concrete example — two people with similar savings but different filing statuses, two portfolios with different risk levels — shows exactly how tax decisions ripple through a retirement plan. This chapter slows down and walks through case studies step by step. None of these is meant as a template to copy blindly — they're illustrations of the principles from earlier chapters, applied to specific numbers, so you can recognize your own situation in at least one of them and adapt the logic to your own life.

11.1 Single vs. Married Filing Jointly: Tax Outcomes Compared

Consider how two retirees with similar income can face different tax outcomes simply because one files single and the other married filing jointly. The federal system gives married couples broader brackets at most income levels — that often helps, but the way incomes combine can also trigger higher marginal rates, more taxable Social Security, or Medicare surcharges. Compare two fictional retirees: Anna, single, and Mark and Lisa, married.

Anna is 67, single, receiving $30,000 a year from Social Security, a $20,000 pension, and withdrawing $20,000 from her traditional IRA — $70,000 total before taxes. She lives in a state that doesn't tax Social Security but does tax IRA withdrawals as ordinary income. Mark and Lisa, both 67 and married, receive $45,000 in combined Social Security, a $25,000 combined pension, and withdraw $30,000 from their traditional IRAs — $100,000 total, which they need partly because they support an adult child and travel more. These aren't identical dollar amounts, but the comparison is realistic: couples often want or need more income than single retirees, while also benefiting from a broader bracket in many ranges.

Tax Bracket Differences

For Anna as a single filer, the 12% bracket caps out at a much lower income than it does for Mark and Lisa filing jointly. The same additional $10,000 IRA withdrawal can land at a higher marginal rate for Anna than for the couple, depending on where each sits relative to the thresholds. Suppose Anna's taxable income, after the standard deduction, sits near the top of the 12% bracket — an extra $10,000 from her IRA for a home improvement could push part or all of it into the 22% bracket. Mark and Lisa, with their joint standard deduction and wider brackets, might draw the same $10,000 and stay entirely within the 12% bracket.

This bracket-width difference shapes withdrawal sequencing directly. A married couple often has plenty of room to recognize income — IRA withdrawals or Roth conversions — at lower rates, which can encourage accelerating taxable income in years when that space is available. A single retiree has less room before the next rate kicks in, so withdrawals and conversions need more careful sizing. The narrower single brackets make tax smoothing more delicate — you can't simply withdraw more now at low rates, because the low-rate band itself is shallower. This becomes especially relevant once RMDs arrive, often just as a single filer has fewer deductions, smaller brackets, and potentially higher medical expenses that don't fully offset the added income.

Social Security Taxation Variances

Filing status also affects how much of your Social Security is taxable, since the IRS uses provisional income thresholds that are lower for single filers than for married couples. Small changes in other income can pull more Social Security into the taxable column for a single filer faster than for a couple.

Anna's $30,000 of Social Security puts $15,000 into her provisional income calculation. Add her $20,000 pension and $20,000 IRA withdrawal, and she's at $55,000 of provisional income — deep into the range where up to 85% of her benefit becomes taxable, meaning roughly $25,500 of her Social Security ends up in her federal taxable income despite starting out "tax-advantaged" in theory. Mark and Lisa start with $45,000 of Social Security, putting $22,500 into their provisional income; adding their pension and IRA withdrawals brings them to a higher dollar total than Anna, but because the couple's thresholds are more generous, the proportion of their Social Security taxed at the 85% level can end up similar despite their larger benefit.

Here's where the lever becomes visible: if Anna reduces her traditional IRA withdrawal from $20,000 to $10,000 and pulls the other $10,000 from a Roth instead, her provisional income drops and less of her Social Security gets pulled into taxation — a double benefit, since she pays less ordinary tax on the IRA portion and keeps more of her Social Security untaxed at the same time. For a single filer like Anna, this interaction is especially powerful, because the thresholds sit closer to her typical income range to begin with.

Impact on Roth Conversion Strategies

Roth conversions are a primary lifetime tax tool, and filing status shapes their effectiveness directly. Mark and Lisa, with $800,000 combined in traditional IRAs, are concerned about future RMDs pushing them into higher brackets — and about the widow's penalty if one spouse passes away first. RMDs from an $800,000 balance in their early seventies could easily reach $30,000 or more and keep growing. Starting at 65, converting $40,000 a year while their joint income sits in a moderate bracket gradually shrinks that future RMD base; because married brackets allow more income at the same rate than single brackets, they might convert $40,000 or even $60,000 in some years and stay within the 22% bracket.

Contrast Anna, with a $600,000 traditional IRA of her own. As a single filer, her bracket space is tighter — converting $40,000 in one year might push her into a much higher marginal bracket and drive up the taxable portion of her Social Security at the same time. Conversions still make sense for Anna, just in smaller annual doses, timed around unusually low-income years, like the period right before she starts claiming Social Security. She might convert $10,000 to $15,000 a year rather than $40,000, saving larger moves for years when her other income happens to be unusually low.

The lesson: filing status shapes both the size of the conversion "sweet spot" and how urgently it needs to be used. Married couples often have a window while both spouses are alive to leverage wide brackets and protect the surviving spouse from the widow's penalty. Single retirees need to be more selective, but the underlying principle is identical — look ahead to future brackets, RMDs, and Medicare thresholds, not just this year's return.

State Tax Considerations for Singles vs. Couples

State rules can tilt the scales further. Some states exempt retirement income or Social Security per taxpayer; others offer credits that phase out differently for single versus married filers. Imagine State A, where Social Security is fully exempt and each taxpayer over 65 can exclude up to $15,000 of pension or IRA income — a married couple shields up to $30,000 combined, while a single retiree like Anna shields $15,000. The rules don't explicitly favor couples, but two singles living separately could each claim a full $15,000 exclusion, while a married couple receives it collectively. Move Anna from State A to a state where pension income is fully taxable and the brackets are less friendly to singles, and her combined federal-and-state marginal rate on IRA withdrawals could rise significantly. The comparative examples in this chapter should always be read through that state-level lens too, since it can amplify or offset everything the federal comparison shows.

11.2 Portfolio Styles: Conservative vs. Growth-Focused Case Studies

Beyond filing status, how your portfolio is invested is a major driver of your tax picture. A conservative, bond-heavy portfolio throws off ordinary income taxed at your marginal rate; a growth-focused, stock-heavy portfolio produces capital gains and qualified dividends, often taxed at preferential rates or even 0% in some brackets. Asset location — which account type holds which investments — adds another dimension entirely.

Conservative Portfolio: Carol

Carol, 72, runs a conservative approach — $1 million total, roughly 70% bonds and CDs, 30% dividend-paying stocks, with much of the fixed income inside her traditional IRA alongside a substantial bond ladder in a taxable account. She's already taking RMDs, and interest from both tax-deferred and taxable bonds shows up as ordinary income. She needs about $60,000 a year, with Social Security covering $25,000 of it — but her fixed income produces more interest than she actually needs for spending, leading to rising cash balances and unwelcome tax bills.

Carol's challenge is managing ordinary bond income alongside RMDs, since every additional dollar stacks on top of Social Security and pushes more income into higher brackets. A tax-efficient adjustment: shifting some taxable bonds into municipal bonds, assuming her bracket is high enough that the lower yield still produces a better after-tax result, and coordinating CD maturities and bond interest timing with her annual withdrawal plan so she doesn't inadvertently create excess income in heavy-RMD years.

In a concrete year, Carol's projected RMD generates $30,000 — more than she needs from the IRA for spending — while her taxable bond ladder produces another $15,000 in interest. She satisfies most of her spending from the RMD itself, covering the $35,000 gap between Social Security and expenses, and reinvests the extra $10,000 she doesn't need immediately into tax-efficient stock index funds in her taxable account, while shifting future bond purchases toward municipal bonds to reduce ordinary income going forward. Over a few years, this lowers the taxable interest she recognizes and helps keep her marginal rate more stable.

Growth-Focused Portfolio: David

David, 65, runs 80% stock and 20% bonds with a strong growth focus — a large taxable brokerage account with significant embedded long-term gains, a moderate traditional IRA, and a sizable Roth IRA. He needs $90,000 a year; Social Security will eventually cover part of that, but for the first few years he relies primarily on his portfolio.

David funds much of his early retirement spending by selling appreciated stock in his taxable account while staying within the 0% or 15% long-term capital gains brackets, and uses his relatively low ordinary income years to convert part of his traditional IRA to Roth at the same time. Because capital gains are taxed separately from ordinary income, he can blend the two carefully. Sell $70,000 of appreciated stock a year — $40,000 cost basis, $30,000 long-term gain — alongside a $10,000 IRA withdrawal, and that covers $80,000 of need before Social Security starts, with the $30,000 gain potentially falling entirely in the 0% bracket and the $10,000 IRA withdrawal taxed at low ordinary rates. With bracket room remaining, he adds a $20,000 Roth conversion on top, filling out the rest of a favorable ordinary bracket without touching the rate on his capital gains. Over several years, these partial conversions shrink his future RMDs and build a tax-free Roth pool to draw from later.

David's pattern is a different kind of tax planning from Carol's — rather than fighting ordinary bond income and RMDs, he spends down taxable equities strategically, harvests gains in low-income years, and times conversions to coincide with market dips or modest-income years.

Balancing Withdrawals Across Account Types

Both retirees must coordinate taxable, tax-deferred, and tax-free withdrawals, but their portfolio styles pull them in different directions. Carol's sequence: satisfy RMDs from the IRA first, use taxable bond interest and maturing CDs for additional cash needs second, sell taxable equity positions third if still short, and treat Roth as a reserve for large one-off expenses or late-life flexibility. David's sequence is more dynamic — emphasizing taxable brokerage withdrawals and capital gain harvesting early, using Roth and IRA withdrawals sparingly at first, then beginning modest IRA withdrawals or conversions as RMD age approaches, with his Roth account serving as both a growth engine and a future tax-free source especially valuable in years he wants higher cash flow without triggering IRMAA or higher brackets.

These patterns tie directly back to Chapter 4's withdrawal sequencing — there's no single "right" order, only the order that fits your account balances, portfolio style, and the external thresholds for Social Security, Medicare, and tax brackets that apply to your situation specifically.

Risk Tolerance Changes Over Time: Emily

Risk tolerance doesn't stay constant through retirement, and tax strategy should evolve alongside it. Emily retires at 60 with a growth-oriented portfolio much like David's. In her first decade, she leans on taxable equity sales and partial Roth conversions, using the same principles above. By her early seventies, less comfortable with market volatility, she's gradually increased her bond allocation — and more of her income now takes the form of interest and RMDs, echoing Carol's situation instead.

In her early years, Emily's tax focus is taking advantage of low ordinary income to convert traditional IRA funds to Roth and realize long-term gains at favorable rates, watching her MAGI carefully to avoid pushing too much future Social Security into taxable territory or triggering IRMAA once Medicare starts. As her Roth balance grows substantial, she begins treating it as a flexible resource for unexpected costs or years she'd rather not sell equities at a loss. By her late seventies, her remaining traditional IRA has been whittled down through earlier conversions and withdrawals, but RMDs are still a factor — her bonds now sit primarily inside the IRA where interest is shielded until withdrawn, while her taxable account holds broad-market equity funds and some municipal bonds. Her focus at this stage is minimizing spikes: coordinating QCDs to reduce taxable RMD income, and using her Roth pool selectively so she doesn't need to increase IRA withdrawals just to fund larger expenses. Her trajectory shows how a retiree can move from a growth-first, conversion-heavy strategy to a more conservative, preservation-oriented one without losing sight of the tax implications at each stage.

11.3 Medicare and IRMAA Impact: Reduction Strategies in Practice

The final set of case studies centers on IRMAA specifically — and how decisions made years before Medicare enrollment ripple into premiums long after the fact, because of the two-year lookback.

Timing Withdrawals: Karen and Michael

Karen and Michael, both 64, will enroll in Medicare at 65 and have been warned about IRMAA. Their plan calls for $120,000 of annual spending, funded by modest pensions, IRA withdrawals, and a taxable brokerage account. They're considering a large home renovation that, if funded entirely through IRA withdrawals, could push that year's income far above the IRMAA line.

Their usual pattern draws about $60,000 from IRAs and $20,000 from taxable accounts. Adding a $70,000 renovation withdrawal would push total IRA withdrawals to $130,000, sharply raising their MAGI — and crossing an IRMAA threshold by even one dollar can trigger hundreds or thousands in higher premiums per person, per year, once they reach Medicare age. Instead, they spread the renovation over two calendar years, funding part with built-up taxable savings and part with more moderate IRA withdrawals each year, scheduling the larger withdrawal for a year when other income happens to be lower. This keeps their MAGI under the relevant threshold in both years and could save them several thousand dollars in avoidable surcharges over their Medicare enrollment, without reducing their lifestyle at all.

Roth Conversions and IRMAA: Paul

Paul, 62, anticipates high RMDs later and wants to use his current lower bracket to convert — but converting too aggressively right around Medicare enrollment could push his MAGI above multiple IRMAA thresholds, offsetting some of the tax benefit with higher premiums. He holds $1.2 million in traditional IRAs with no pension income, expects Social Security to start at 67, and knows RMDs become mandatory in his early seventies.

Starting at 63, rather than converting $200,000 in a single year — which would unquestionably spike his income — Paul models $50,000 conversions annually across six years. In the first two years, before Medicare begins, he has more freedom to let MAGI run higher if he's comfortable with the tax bill. Once he turns 65, he reduces the annual conversion amount to stay within whatever IRMAA threshold corresponds to a premium level he's willing to pay. These "serial conversions" substantially lower his traditional IRA balance over time, shrinking both future RMDs and the ordinary income that would otherwise show up on his return in his seventies and beyond — trading some tax and IRMAA cost now for more control later, rather than letting the system impose large forced distributions when he has fewer options left.

Coordinating Taxable and Tax-Deferred Sources: Susan

A common mistake is treating each account type in isolation — spend taxable first, then the IRA, save Roth for last — without factoring in IRMAA's stair-step structure. Susan, 70, already on Medicare for several years, has a taxable brokerage account, a traditional IRA, and a Roth IRA. Her baseline spending including taxes and healthcare runs $80,000 a year: Social Security covers $30,000, and she typically draws $30,000 from her IRA and $20,000 from taxable investments, keeping her MAGI comfortably below the first IRMAA threshold most years.

One year, she sells a rental property with a large capital gain that alone would push her into multiple higher IRMAA tiers. To soften the impact, she reduces her IRA withdrawal that year to the bare RMD minimum, relying more on taxable cash reserves and, if needed, her Roth for spending — since the property sale already raised her income enough on its own. In a different year with no large sale or unusual income, she reverses the pattern: a larger IRA withdrawal to address RMD obligations, modest taxable account sales to top up spending, Roth left untouched. This kind of year-by-year coordination, projecting income before making big moves, prevents stepping unnecessarily into the next IRMAA tier — sometimes accepting a slightly higher tax bill in one year specifically to avoid a multi-year pattern of higher premiums.

Reviewing IRMAA After Life Events

Even with careful planning, life happens. Maria and James, a married couple in their early seventies, have paid IRMAA surcharges for years because James continued consulting work at a high income. When James unexpectedly becomes ill and stops working, their income drops dramatically — but the Medicare notices they receive still reflect the older, higher income from two years prior. Rather than accepting the higher premiums, they gather documentation of the life-changing event — proof of work stoppage — and submit a request for IRMAA reconsideration. The process involves a specific form, selecting the type of life-changing event, and supporting documents like tax returns or employer letters; their reconsideration is approved, and their IRMAA tier adjusts downward to match their new income.

A related scenario plays out for Ellen, a widow whose husband passed away the previous year. Her filing status shifts from married filing jointly to single, shrinking some deductions and brackets — but her household income doesn't fall immediately, since she still has RMDs and investment income continuing as before. This can push her into a higher IRMAA tier as a single filer even though her lifestyle hasn't really changed. If her income shortly after her spouse's death is genuinely lower than the income from two years earlier, she too can request reconsideration based on the life event of losing a spouse.

These examples point to a broader theme running through this entire chapter: retirement taxes aren't static. Filing status, portfolio style, income sources, and Medicare rules interact continuously, shifting in response to both your deliberate choices and events outside your control. Working through detailed scenarios like these is how you learn to recognize where the actual levers sit — which account to draw from, when to time a conversion, how to manage bracket thresholds, when to use an appeal process — and how to pull them deliberately instead of reactively. Find the elements that match your own situation among Anna, Mark and Lisa, Carol, David, Emily, and the Medicare-focused examples, and you have a working starting point for building your own tax-efficient path.

Key Takeaways

• Filing status changes the math directly: married filing jointly brackets are wider, giving couples more room to convert or withdraw at a given rate than a single filer with the same income

• Single filers hit Social Security taxation thresholds at lower income levels than married couples, making the IRA-versus-Roth withdrawal choice more powerful for them specifically

• A conservative, bond-heavy portfolio fights ordinary income and RMDs; a growth-focused, equity-heavy portfolio manages capital gains and conversion timing instead — the right sequencing strategy depends on which situation you're actually in

• Risk tolerance and tax strategy both evolve through retirement — a plan built at 60 should look different by 75, even without any external rule forcing the change

• IRMAA's two-year lookback means a decision at 63 can affect a premium at 65, and a decision at 68 can still affect a premium at 70

• A genuine life-changing event (death of a spouse, work stoppage) can justify an IRMAA reconsideration request — most retirees who qualify never ask

Chapter 12: Choosing Advisors and Ongoing Learning: Staying Tax-Savvy in Retirement

Chapter at a Glance

What you'll learn in this chapter:

• The difference between a fiduciary advisor and one held only to a "suitability" standard — and the exact question that reveals which one you're talking to

• What "fee-only" actually means, and why it matters more in retirement tax planning than almost anywhere else

• The red flags that signal an advisor's incentives don't match your interests

• A repeatable system for staying current on tax law changes without turning into a part-time tax researcher

Estimated reading time: 23 minutes

> ***FIELD NOTE*** *The best advisor relationship in the world can't save you from a tax law that changes five years after you retire if nobody's paying attention. And the most diligent self-education can't replace good judgment from someone who's seen a thousand retirements, not just your own. This chapter is about building both halves at once.*

Most people think of "doing taxes" as something that happens once a year with a stack of forms. By retirement, taxes become less of an annual chore and more of an ongoing part of financial life — income sources change, spending evolves, and the rules themselves never stop shifting. The strategy you build in your sixties may need rethinking in your seventies, and again in your eighties.

This chapter is about keeping that strategy alive: choosing the right advisors, and building a simple system for lifelong learning. The goal isn't turning you into a tax attorney — it's becoming the kind of retiree who knows when to get help, how to evaluate it, and how to stay informed enough to spot when your plan needs an update.

12.1 Finding and Evaluating Fiduciary, Fee-Only Advisors

Understanding Fiduciary Duty

A crucial distinction in the advisory world: fiduciary versus non-fiduciary. A fiduciary is legally obligated to put your interests ahead of their own — which sounds obvious, but isn't the default standard in the financial industry. Many people calling themselves "financial advisors" operate under a suitability standard instead, meaning they must recommend something "suitable," not necessarily the best or least expensive option available to you.

A fiduciary advisor must be prepared to show their recommendations serve your best interest even when it means earning less themselves — disclosing conflicts of interest, explaining compensation clearly, documenting their reasoning. Someone bound only by suitability can steer you toward a higher-commission product as long as it isn't obviously inappropriate. This difference matters enormously in retirement, when complex products like annuities and managed accounts are on the table and tax considerations can tilt the balance between approaches.

You don't have to guess. Ask directly: "Will you act as a fiduciary to me at all times, for all of the services you provide?" Follow up by asking them to confirm that commitment in writing, usually in their client agreement or Form ADV brochure. Many fee-only registered investment advisors and CFP® professionals will state this clearly and without hesitation. If an advisor hedges, gives a vague answer, or says they're a fiduciary "sometimes" or "when managing investments but not when selling insurance," that's a signal to probe deeper or move on.

The Fee-Only Compensation Model

The second filter is how the advisor is paid. "Fee-only" means compensation comes exclusively from the fees you pay — not commissions or kickbacks tied to specific products — whether charged as a percentage of assets managed, a flat annual fee, or hourly. Fee-only doesn't automatically mean cheap, and it doesn't automatically mean hourly either; many fee-only firms work on an ongoing AUM basis.

This matters specifically for retirement tax planning because taxes interact with nearly every product decision. The temptation to push a higher-commission annuity or an expensive proprietary fund weakens considerably when the advisor's pay doesn't change based on what they sell you — you're paying for judgment and planning, not for someone's ability to move product. When interviewing prospective advisors, ask plainly: "How do you get paid in our relationship — by me, by product companies, or both?" and "If I follow your recommended plan, what will my total annual costs be, including advisory fees and typical investment expenses?" Ask them to illustrate with dollar amounts, not just percentages — "On a $750,000 portfolio, what would my annual fee be, and what additional fund expenses would I likely pay?" Be cautious of any structure where the advisor's pay spikes when you buy a particular investment or insurance policy; that's not inherently disqualifying, but it adds a conflict you need to navigate consciously.

Interviewing and Vetting Prospects

Once you've narrowed to fiduciary, fee-only candidates, assess both technical competence and human fit — retirement tax planning isn't just math, it's an ongoing relationship around some of the most personal parts of your life. Prepare questions specific to retirement and taxes, not just investing: "What experience do you have with clients recently retired or within ten years of retirement?" "How do you model different Social Security claiming strategies for married couples?" "How do you evaluate whether Roth conversions make sense for a client in their sixties or seventies?" "What tools do you use to project taxes over the next 20 to 30 years?"

Check credentials beyond content expertise — CFP®, CPA, Chartered Retirement Planning Counselor, Retirement Income Certified Professional, or Chartered Financial Consultant all indicate formal education and ongoing continuing education in planning topics, and many can be verified through regulatory databases. Ask for references with a profile similar to yours, and ask those references what the advisor is like in a crisis, how responsive they are, and whether tax issues come up proactively or only when the client raises them. Pay attention to how complex ideas get explained — dense jargon, or a clear explanation of Roth conversion timing and IRMAA that actually makes sense to you? The relationship only works if you feel comfortable asking "basic" questions and getting straightforward answers. Notice the tone too: do they ask about your values and goals, or jump straight to investment returns? A tax-savvy retirement plan is built around your life — spending, health expectations, legacy wishes — not just your rate of return.

Recognizing Red Flags and Sales Pressure

Aggressive product pushing is the clearest red flag — if conversations revolve around a particular annuity, proprietary fund, or insurance policy rather than your goals and broader plan, be cautious. So is any guarantee of unusually high returns or promises you'll "never lose money" without a clear explanation of trade-offs and costs. In the tax space specifically, be wary of anyone claiming they can "eliminate" your taxes rather than manage and minimize them within the rules that actually exist.

Lack of transparency is another concern — vagueness or defensiveness about fees, conflicts of interest, or regulatory record is a problem; a trustworthy advisor welcomes questions about their Form ADV and compensation structure. Pay attention to how you feel during the meeting too. Rushed, talked over, nudged to sign before you've had time to think? Healthy advisory relationships feel collaborative — you should feel heard, not managed. If you walk away uneasy, trust that instinct. You can always keep looking.

12.2 Keeping Plans Current with Law Changes and Inflation Adjustments

Choosing a good advisor is only part of the story. The other part is building a rhythm for updating your plan as the world shifts — brackets change, deductions and credits adjust, Medicare premiums move, and your own spending, health, and family circumstances aren't static either.

Scheduling Annual Reviews

Treat your retirement tax strategy as a living document. At least once a year — perhaps every fall, before year-end decisions lock in — review income sources, spending, investment performance, and current tax rules together. The real question isn't "how did our returns do," it's "given what's changed, do we still have the right withdrawal strategy, are we in the right brackets, do our conversion plans still make sense?" Revisit your withdrawal sequencing, confirm actual income is on track with the projected bracket, and look one or two years ahead at how upcoming RMDs, pension starts, or annuity payments will alter the picture.

Include life changes explicitly in the review — marriage, divorce, death of a spouse, the sale of a home, a large charitable gift, a significant health event. If you work with an advisor and they rarely update projections or adjust to new tax laws, that's a sign their service level may not match the complexity your situation actually has. The annual review is also the natural checkpoint to evaluate whether your advisor relationship still fits — if your needs have grown more complex, or you want deeper coordination across estate planning and charitable giving, this is the moment to raise it and see how they respond.

Tracking Inflation and Cost-of-Living Adjustments

Inflation isn't obviously a tax topic, but it becomes one quickly in retirement. As living costs rise, many tax parameters adjust too — standard deductions, bracket thresholds, sometimes income ranges for credits or surcharges — and Social Security benefits typically receive annual cost-of-living adjustments as well. All of this interacts with your withdrawal strategy directly. Higher spending needs from inflation mean larger withdrawals, which can push you into a higher bracket or trigger additional premiums down the line; but if brackets also adjust upward with inflation, you may temporarily have more room for conversions or favorable-rate gain realization. Part of staying tax-savvy is noticing when these windows open and closing them deliberately rather than by accident.

During your annual review, update your budget using actual inflation data for your main cost categories, compare it with how your withdrawals have changed, and check how inflation has shifted the thresholds that matter to you — the standard deduction, the 0% capital gains bracket, your target bracket breakpoints. If Social Security COLA increases are pushing your taxable income up on their own, you may need to trim withdrawals elsewhere to stay in your preferred bracket. This feeds directly into the long-term stress-testing from earlier chapters — projecting 20 or 30 years of retirement income with realistic inflation assumptions is critical to seeing whether your plan can deliver the after-tax income you need without depleting assets too quickly.

Monitoring Medicare and IRMAA Changes

Medicare premiums function as a quiet tax on higher-income retirees, and the thresholds that trigger IRMAA can shift over time while always reflecting income from two years prior. If you're doing large conversions, realizing big gains, or taking large one-time withdrawals, you may inadvertently cross into a higher IRMAA tier — raising Medicare costs for a year or more, sometimes outweighing whatever tax benefit motivated the move in the first place. Every year, the Centers for Medicare & Medicaid Services announces updated premiums and IRMAA brackets — make checking those numbers part of your annual review. Ask directly: given our expected MAGI two years from now, are we at risk of crossing into a higher tier, and if so, do we want to accelerate or defer certain income events to control that? Aligning withdrawal and conversion plans with IRMAA deserves the same attention as aligning them with tax brackets.

Leveraging Reliable Resources for Updates

You don't need to read the Internal Revenue Code to stay current, but a few dependable sources help. Government sources — IRS publications and announcements, Social Security and Medicare websites, official state tax sites — are the backbone, providing the raw information on new thresholds and rule changes. Complement those with reputable financial publications that translate changes into plain-language implications for retirees, and consider a newsletter from a fee-only advisory firm or nonprofit financial education organization that highlights practical takeaways rather than chasing every headline. If you work with an advisor, ask how they stay on top of changes and how they communicate updates to clients — periodic updates, special meetings when major legislation passes — so you know someone is responsible for turning new information into specific recommendations for your situation.

12.3 Ongoing Resources, FAQs, and Next Steps for Lifelong Learning

Once you have a trustworthy advisor and a habit of regular reviews, the final ingredient is your own learning process — a light-touch practice of staying curious and asking good questions, not studying tax code late into the night.

Creating a Personal Learning Routine

Treat this like preventive healthcare: periodic checkups and modest ongoing maintenance, rather than waiting until something's badly wrong. An hour once a month or once a quarter, spent reading or watching something specifically about retirement taxes and planning, is enough. Over time, terms like "bracket creep," "Roth conversion ladder," "qualified charitable distribution," or "IRMAA" become familiar, and familiarity with the language makes it easier to ask targeted questions and spot when something in your life might affect your strategy. The goal is consistency, not intensity.

Engaging with Online Tools and Calculators

Experimenting with reliable calculators using your own numbers makes abstract concepts feel concrete. Start with simple questions — "If I withdraw an extra $10,000 from my IRA this year, how does that affect my marginal rate?" or "How would converting $25,000 a year for five years change my taxes now and later?" — then gradually explore more advanced scenarios combining Social Security, pension income, and part-time work. These tools rely on simplified assumptions and won't be perfect, but they're genuinely useful for building intuition, and bringing the results to your advisor — "the calculator suggests small conversions now keep my future RMDs and IRMAA lower; do you agree, and if not, what are we assuming differently?" — makes for a sharper, more productive conversation. Treat them as conversation starters, not final verdicts.

Addressing Frequently Asked Questions

Even engaged retirees circle back to the same handful of questions repeatedly. Rather than memorizing every rule, it's more useful to know where to find clear, trustworthy answers when they arise — government FAQs from the IRS or Social Security Administration, plus educational content from major financial institutions, tend to be reliable starting points. Common recurring themes: when RMDs start for a specific account type and what happens if you miss one; what portion of Social Security is taxable at different income levels and how other income affects that; whether there's a "best age" for Roth conversions and how to weigh short-term cost against long-term benefit. Watch for explanations that use clear examples rather than heavy jargon — those are the ones that translate cleanly to your own situation. If an answer stays unclear or the rules seem contradictory, bring it to your advisor; a good fiduciary is used to navigating nuance and explaining the "why," not just the "what."

Seeking Community and Professional Support

It's easy to feel alone in retirement decisions, especially ones involving taxes. Retiree forums, local financial education workshops, and discussion groups through community centers or libraries can make the learning process more sustainable — as can online communities, with a healthy skepticism and a habit of verifying specific recommendations with a professional before acting on them. Hearing how other retirees approach Social Security timing or sudden medical expenses can surface questions you didn't know to ask. At the same time, recognize the limits of peer advice — what worked for someone in a different bracket, different state, or different health situation may not transfer to you, which is exactly where a long-term relationship with a fee-only fiduciary advisor earns its value: someone who knows your history and can help adapt your strategy as laws, markets, and family circumstances change.

Think of your tax strategy going forward as a partnership between three elements: your own growing knowledge, the tools you use to experiment and learn, and the advisors and communities around you. You don't need perfection. You need a direction, a process, and a team — formal and informal — that help you stick to sound principles while staying flexible. Choose your advisors thoughtfully, review your plan regularly, and stay curious enough to keep learning, and you'll be well positioned for whatever the tax landscape looks like in the decades ahead.

Key Takeaways

• A fiduciary is legally required to put your interests first; an advisor held only to a "suitability" standard is not — ask directly which standard applies to every service they provide

• "Fee-only" means compensation comes solely from client fees, not commissions — this matters most in retirement tax planning, where product incentives and tax efficiency can pull in opposite directions

• Aggressive product pushing, vagueness about fees, and promises to "eliminate" taxes are all genuine red flags worth walking away from

• Schedule one real annual review — ideally every fall — covering income, spending, bracket position, and any life changes before year-end decisions lock in

• Medicare IRMAA brackets and standard deductions are both adjusted for inflation; check both every year rather than assuming last year's numbers still apply

• Ongoing learning doesn't require studying tax code — an hour a month, a couple of reliable sources, and a willingness to ask your advisor "why" is enough to stay genuinely informed

Conclusion

You started this book with a pile of accounts and a vague sense that taxes would eat into them somehow. By now you know exactly how: which dollars are ordinary income, which are capital gains, which are tax-free, and which combination of withdrawals keeps you out of the next bracket instead of stumbling into it.

That's the real shift. Not optimism about retirement — precision about it.

A few things are worth carrying forward. Your withdrawal sequence isn't a one-time decision; it's a yearly one, because your income, the tax law, and your account balances all move. Roth conversions work best in the years your income is unusually low, not on a fixed schedule. IRMAA and RMDs both run on lookback periods, so this year's choices land two years from now — plan with that lag in mind, not against it.

The tax code changes more than people expect. The new senior deduction that applies through 2028, inflation-adjusted IRMAA brackets, QCD limits that rise most years — none of this is static, which is exactly why a once-a-year review matters more than a perfect plan made once and left alone.

Before you close this book, a short checklist:

- Map your expected income and withdrawals for the next twelve months
- Check where that income falls relative to your tax bracket and the IRMAA thresholds
- Revisit any Roth conversion plans against this year's actual numbers, not last year's
- If you give to charity and you're 70½ or older, compare a QCD against writing a check
- Put one date on the calendar — a real one — for your annual tax review

You don't need to become a tax professional. You need a process you'll actually repeat. That's what this book was for.

Thank you for spending the time on this. Most retirees never look past the headline rules. You went further.

Free Tools From Essential Retirement Guide

Five free calculators built to go alongside this series — no signup required to see your results.

Visit **essentialretirementguide.com** or scan any code below to open a tool on your phone or computer.

Roth Conversion Calculator — What's My Sweet Spot?
Find the maximum you can convert from a traditional IRA to a Roth this year without pushing income into a higher tax bracket. Uses the actual 2026 IRS federal tax brackets.

https://www.essentialretirementguide.com/roth-calc

Social Security Tax Calculator — How Much of My Benefit Is Taxable?
Enter your income and filing status to see exactly how much of your Social Security benefit is subject to federal tax, based on the IRS provisional income formula.

https://www.essentialretirementguide.com/tax-calc

RMD Calculator — What's My Required Minimum Distribution?
Find out exactly how much you're required to withdraw this year, when your deadline is, and what the penalty looks like if you miss it. Based on the IRS Uniform Lifetime Table for 2026.

https://www.essentialretirementguide.com/rmd

Early Withdrawal Penalty Calculator — What Would This Really Cost Me?
See the actual dollar cost of taking money out of a 401(k) or IRA before age 59½ — penalty and tax combined. Includes seven IRS penalty exceptions including the Rule of 55 and SEPP.

https://www.essentialretirementguide.com/penalty-calc

Social Security Claiming Age Calculator — When Should I File?
Compare your monthly benefit at age 62, your Full Retirement Age, and age 70 — and see which filing age gives you the most lifetime income based on your life expectancy.

https://www.essentialretirementguide.com/ss-calc

All tools are free to use. A personalized PDF report is available by email after you see your results.

Further Reading

This book draws on publicly available government and financial-industry sources. If you want to dig into the official rules yourself, these are the best places to start:

IRS — Retirement Plan and IRA Required Minimum Distributions FAQs

irs.gov/retirement-plans/retirement-plan-and-ira-required-minimum-distributions-faqs

IRS Publication 915 — Social Security and Equivalent Railroad Retirement Benefits

irs.gov/publications/p915

Social Security Administration — Benefit Taxation and COLA Information

ssa.gov

Medicare.gov — Part B and Part D Costs

medicare.gov/basics/costs

CMS — Medicare Parts A & B Premiums and Deductibles (updated annually)

cms.gov

Figures and thresholds in this book reflect 2026 rules and are updated annually for inflation. Always confirm current numbers before making a decision, since IRMAA brackets, contribution limits, and deduction amounts change every year.

Next in The Essential Retirement Strategy Series

THE ESSENTIAL RETIREMENT INCOME BLUEPRINT

How to Turn Your Retirement Savings Into Lasting Income

Saving for retirement is only half the journey—knowing how to turn those savings into reliable income is what truly determines long-term financial security. Yet many retirees reach this stage without a clear plan for how their money will support them over time.

The Essential Retirement Income Strategy Guide focuses on one of the most critical aspects of retirement planning: converting accumulated savings into sustainable income that lasts throughout your lifetime.

Inside this upcoming guide, you'll learn how to:

• Understand the key sources of retirement income, including Social Security, pensions, and investment accounts
• Create a strategy to turn savings into consistent monthly income
• Balance stability, growth, and flexibility in your retirement plan
• Navigate risks like market volatility, inflation, and increasing life expectancy

This practical guide will help you confidently transition from saving to spending, giving you a clearer path toward a stable and reliable retirement income.

Expanding in 2026